The combination of biblical
life stories will leave you craving ...
makes the doors that the Bible presents understand-
able, but also relatable. *Through the Door* will leave you
feeling capable to move forward in your life, knowing
that God is with you every step of the way.

—Kary Oberbrunner, author of
Your Secret Name and *The Deeper Path*

Pastor Tom Pendergrass' first foray into the world of
publishing is a wonderful addition to the library of medi-
tations. *Through the Door* is a rich collection of personal
anecdotes into which he weaves life lessons. Each day's
devotion is thought provoking, biblically sound, and
Tom's down-home honesty and sense of humor shine
through. As I read his personal stories, I wondered if
I would have had the courage to reveal as much. Tom
made me look at myself and apply what he terms "transformational truths" to push open a door from my past.
Doing so has been revealing and refreshing.

—David G Hansen, PhD, COL (Ret) USA,
author of *In Their Sandals: How His Followers Saw
Jesus* and coauthor of *A Visual Guide to Bible Events*
and *A Visual Guide to Gospel Events*

Some books *may* eventually make it onto a shelf. Tom's
work *had* to be written. His life experience has been a
book in waiting. The Apostle Paul told the Corinthians
that their "lives were letters." Tom's life is a letter
penned to all of us, who need to read it. Get this book,
read it, meditate on it, and become more like Jesus!

—Dean Fulks, author of *Your Next 30 Days*
and Pastor of Lifepoint Church

Tom Pendergrass has a close walk with Jesus and it shows in this book! While we all can relate to Tom's life experiences, Tom takes it to the next level by helping us see things through biblical applications. Tom does a great job helping us realize that the Lord is at work in the real world. The reader will identify through Tom's humor, wit, and keen ability to tell a story. The spiritual punch soon follows that will have you thinking, reflecting, and bringing life change to attitudes as well as behaviors. Let Tom take you on a 40-day experience that will be a blessing to you!

—Mark Snowden,
Director of Missional Leadership CABA

Some people have "it," others get "it," and there are a few that have "it" and get "it" like Pastor Tom Pendergrass. In Tom's book *Through the Door* Tom writes like a pastor who has "it" (a personal relationship with God) and a person who gets "it" (what a personal relationship with God means in our daily lives).

—Mark Wilson,
Senior Pastor of North Fairfield Baptist Church

Opening the door to Jesus as Lord and Savior is only the first of many doors we encounter in our Christian walk. God invites us to follow Him to places and people that, on our own, we might not ever choose to experience. Which door are you avoiding? What's keeping you from stepping through? Don't let fear, intimidation, or apathy keep you on the other side of what God has for you. He wants to use you and grow you in amazing ways, but the first step is turning that doorknob and giving it a push. *Through the Door* will help you discover what God has for you and the courage to move forward in faith.

—Kevin Ezell, President of NAMB

I have known Pastor Tom for a number of years and regard him as a great mentor. Every time I have sat and listened to him share about the greatest passion of his life, Jesus, I have come away enriched and standing a bit taller in my walk with Jesus. This book is no different and it is exciting to read the heart of one of my heroes of faith.

—John Palandri, Director of Global Operations & Missions and Challenge Newspaper

Pastor Tom Pendergrass is one of the most humble and genuine men I have ever known. His book, *Through the Door,* is an encouraging, challenging, and transformative 40-day journey for any person seeking to deepen their walk with Jesus. Take the time to read this book and learn from someone who writes from personal experience.

—Aaron Taylor, Teaching Pastor of Living Hope Church

Knowing the heart of Brother Tom and what he writes he lives, I am happy to endorse his book.

—Harold Peasley, Church Planter Mentor of NAMB

I am so grateful that Pastor Tom has pushed open the closed door of fear and failure and into the freedom of writing this 40 day devotional, *Through the Door*. I love the way it is structured with thought provoking scripture, commentary, and reflection questions that take you into the heart of the particular "door" being highlighted. For years, Pastor Tom has pointed me to Jesus through his preaching, counsel and friendship. It is exciting to think of this devotional book pointing thousands to Jesus through his writing. Tom has a unique way of bringing his real-life experiences to the analogies of the doors we encounter in life. The transformational truths found in each day's lesson causes you to ponder the deeper things of life. God has used Pastor Tom to encourage, challenge, and motivate me in life. This book is just another example of that. I love you Pastor Tom. You have been and will continue to be a model and inspiration for me and my family. As you once told me, "Don't keep the faith....give it away!"

—Randy Hepner,
AIA Campus Field Ministry Director

I have known Tom Pendergrass for many years and it is with great pleasure I commend his first book to you. I am confident you will find what he has to say both a challenge and a blessing. I can assure you that his writing is not some theoretical material, but comes out of the coal face of his Christian walk, where, over the years he has faced many struggles and challenges in his personal and pastoral ministry.

—Carl Carmody,
Challenge Newspaper

THROUGH
—— THE ——
DOOR

40 DAYS TO CLOSE THE DOORS OF YOUR PAST,
OPEN THE DOOR TO YOUR FUTURE,
AND TRANSFORM YOUR LIFE

TOM PENDERGRASS

Published by Author Academy Elite
P.O. Box 43, Powell, OH 43035
www.AuthorAcademyElite.com

Cover Design: 99designs
Interior Design: Jetlaunch
Editor: Alex Farmer

Paperback ISBN: 978-1-64085-489-5
Hardcover ISBN: 978-1-64085-490-1
Ebook: 978-1-64085-491-8

Library of Congress Control Number: 2018963612

Available in hardcover, softcover, e-book, and audiobook

For Donna.
My best friend and wife of forty-two years. You motivate, challenge, hold me accountable, and humble me all at the same time. I still smile when you walk into the room!
I love you more today than the day I met you.

CONTENTS

.

FOREWORD

I can't even begin to number the doors that I have walked in and out of through my life. Some doors I ran to full speed ahead, excited for the new adventure they held. While others, I worked hard to leave behind and never open again.

Tom Pendergrass' devotional, *Through the Door*, addresses all of the doors that God has placed in our lives. Within the first few pages, you will find Tom's down to earth personality completely relatable and endearing. His overwhelming love for Jesus will leave an impact on your heart as he shares the way God has changed his life.

Tom and I have served in ministry together for almost 20 years. I've watched firsthand as he has led our church to clearly see where God would open doors of opportunity. I have also witnessed Tom's leadership in walking believers through the difficulty of doors that close and the response that followers of Christ should rest in.

This book removes any notion that we are alone in the trials and successes we meet. We all face the open door, the door of fellowship, and the door of adversity, whether we want to or not. The "transformational truths" that Tom provides in each chapter will show you how to welcome new doors, and overcome others that can cause pain and suffering.

Through the use of biblical truths, scripture, stories, and personal experience, Tom leads you on a path that can help you to take that next step forward to change your life. What you discover in this book will cause you to look at past events from a new perspective. You will know that you can walk into your future prepared because Jesus will be walking with you. This does not mean that life will always be easy, but it reminds us that we are never asked to walk through any door alone. All you need to do is let Him lead.

Come on in, and welcome to the next 40 days *Through The Door*!

David Bickers
Worship Pastor, Urbancrest

INTRODUCTION

There have been a lot of events in my life that will be both a first and last moment. These are the kind of events that you will only experience one time. I can distinctly remember spiraling down the Sangha River in the Democratic Republic of Congo thinking, "What am I doing in this river in a hollowed-out log?" With perfect clarity, I recall walking on a Safari through the river for about a half-mile, only to be told by our guide that "the alligators weren't aggressive!" Definitely a first and last moment.

I once was a passenger in a helicopter that flew into an active volcano. As we were flying, the pilot told us that a film crew had gone down in this volcano less than six months ago. Only one man survived the night and wasn't rescued until the next day. As we hovered over a 2,000-degree lava pool, I felt paralyzed after hearing the pilot say, "We will hover for about fifteen seconds, so have your cameras ready. After fifteen seconds, the paint begins to melt off the helicopter." Another first, that I never plan on experiencing again.

As heart-pounding as those events were (and still are), the thought of writing a book intimidated me more. To write is to become vulnerable to the reality that this could be a tremendous flop. What if I hadn't heard clearly from the Lord to write words of encouragement? After kicking this can down the road for about fifteen years, I'm stepping out of the boat to walk in uncharted waters. I pray that I will keep my eyes fixed on Jesus and that He will speak through me to edify the body of Christ.

Through the Door was born out of a sermon series I preached at Urbancrest in February of 2004. We relocated our campus to a seventy-acre corn field, and God was moving in an incredible way. For thirteen straight Sundays, I spoke on the subject of "Doors in Scripture." During those weeks, we saw sixty-nine first time professions of faith with multiple people filling our altars and being set free. Souls were saved, marriages were healed, and hope was given to many who had lost vision for their lives.

At that time, I was encouraged by many to write a book surrounding this subject. I never picked up a pen due to the fear of being a failure. Here's what I've learned since; "You never fail when you share Jesus." As you meditate upon this book, know that we are fellow pilgrims on a journey. A journey to be set free. Freedom comes through the doors that scripture provides. There are doors that we open, and there are doors we are warned never to walk through. Some doors, only God can reveal and open for us.

For years, I have let the door of fear and failure keep me from writing. I have pushed through the door and am willing to allow God to do what I, in myself, think is impossible. As we journey through the door of salvation and come face-to-face with the door of the tomb, I pray that many will be spiritually set free. Cherish the fact that we've been forgiven and redeemed. We hear the plea of Jesus, as He knocks on the door, and calls out our name. He is asking us to open the door of our heart and renew our fellowship with Him. There are doors of adversity, opportunity, and warning all designed for our spiritual edification as we glorify Christ in our daily walk.

Forty days from now, I am praying that all stress and anxiety will be lifted. I pray that we represent Christ as we walk through doors that we never even knew existed. Doors to mature and protect us. Let the new chapter of our lives begin! If you believe that the door to His presence has been closed, keep reading. He loves you more than you could ever know and His grace is greater than you could have ever dreamed. It's waiting on the other side of the door. Choose to take this journey forward, through the door.

Pastor Tom Pendergrass

I

THE OPEN DOOR

Revelation 3:7-13

Founded in 189 BC, the city of Philadelphia was known for being a powerful trading hub. Citizens walked through prosperous streets filled with glorious and elaborate temples. Earthquakes left the city in shambles, but ruins of those once spectacular buildings can still be seen today. Citizens implemented and quickly adapted to Greek culture by speaking their language and worshiping pagan gods. The Church of Philadelphia did not conform to the ways of its city but was filled with a faithful and obedient congregation.

Christ's message to the Church of Philadelphia was full of encouragement and commitment. The church was not large or powerful, but they proved themselves to be faithful. The members of this church practiced His Word, and were rewarded in return with the promise of an eternally "open door". If He opens the doors, you must work. If He shuts the doors, you must wait. Don't miss your opportunity to step through the doors that God opens for you. Over the next five days, you will learn how to apply the faithfulness that the Church of Philadelphia possessed into your own life. Whatever door He opens for you, trust and follow Him.

DAY 1

GETTING ZONKED

"...See, I have set before you an open door,
and no one can shut it..."

Revelation 3:8

As a child, I grew fond of watching *Let's Make a Deal* where contestants win prizes throughout the game show. In the finale, two contestants have the chance to win a prize by choosing between three doors. The contestants must sacrifice their prizes to choose a door, and the participant who gives up the most will have the first choice. Each door contains the possibility of getting "Zonked" where you lose it all in return for a gag prize. On this journey towards transformation, you will face challenges regarding what lies beyond the door. Will you get "Zonked" or will it change the course of your life?

The process of transformation from a babe in Christ to that of spiritual maturity involves countless

3

opportunities and obstacles. Through my life, I have approached a multitude of doors that brought about exciting, new challenges. Each door you enter will come with both positive and negative consequences. How can you unlock the "open door" to make a difference for the Kingdom of God, your family, and yourself?

Ask yourself these principles when taking the next step. Will this door bring honor to the One that is holy and true? Does this door have the affirmation and blessing of Scripture? Does this door require me to rely more on Christ than on my own talent and ability? How will this door be used to further His Kingdom? As the One who is "holy and true," Jesus will always stay consistent. He will never ask you to compromise your character, beliefs, or His Word. The door you choose to walk through never requires you to deny His Name, but to strive to make His fame even greater.

TRANSFORMATIONAL TRUTH:
THEY WERE WEAK, BUT THEY WERE WILLING.

IN REVELATIONS 3:7-13, THE PEOPLE OF THE CHURCH OF PHILADELPHIA HAD A LITTLE STRENGTH. YOUR SMALLNESS IS THAT OF HUMANS, BUT ANY STRENGTH YOU POSSESS IS GOD GIVEN. THE PROCESS OF TRANSFORMATION BEHIND EACH OPEN DOOR FOCUSES ON BEING AVAILABLE. NOT ON MY ABILITY TO CONQUER, BUT TO COMMIT. NOT ON MY RESUME, BUT MY RESOLVE. NOT ON MY FINANCES, BUT MY FAITH. THE MESSAGE TO PHILADELPHIA IS WRITTEN TO ENCOURAGE EACH MEMBER OF THE BODY OF CHRIST TO REST IN CHRIST. WHAT THE WORLD CALLS WEAKNESSES, THE BIBLE CALLS STRENGTHS. THERE ARE NO WORDS OF CONDEMNATION GIVEN. INSTEAD, YOU RECEIVE AN

INVITATION TO JOIN CHRIST THROUGH THE DOORS THAT ONLY HE CAN OPEN. WHEN GOD INVITES YOU TO JOIN HIM, HE SAYS THAT ALL THE ASSETS, ARSENAL, ANGELS, AND AUTHORITY OF HEAVEN ARE AT YOUR DISPOSAL. THROUGH YOUR WEAKNESS YOU WALK THROUGH THE DOORS HE OPENS.

As you face your next step towards spiritual transformation what doors are before you? Is it a career decision? Is it a commitment to your future husband or wife? Is it the church you will invest your life in as they invest in you spiritually? Is it deciding which college to attend, where you will give the next four or more years of your life? Day one teaches you to rely on His strength and provision, not your own. Rely upon His Word and His promises as you walk by faith and not sight. Make the Name of Jesus something precious.

REFLECT

Will the door you're getting ready to walk through bring glory and honor to your Savior and family?

Have you sought direction and affirmation through His Word, His Spirit, and through your family of Faith?

Are you prepared to face the challenges that will certainly result from opening this door?

DAY 2

OPPORTUNITY OF FAITH

*"…You used what little strength you had
to keep My Word…"*

Revelation 3:8 (MSG)

The church at Philadelphia was commended for having kept God's Word. In return, He promises that no one could shut the doors that He opens, no matter what obstacles you may face. There are three types of obstacles that define your spiritual growth. 1) God uses trials to test your faith. 2) You create obstacles when you focus on yourself instead of abiding with Christ and the grace He provides. 3) You will receive external challenges which are created by opposition from others. God promises to walk with you each step of every day and to take care of your enemies, both human and demonic. The open door He provides, requires you to rest in Him to rely upon His strength not your own.

"Casting all your cares upon Him, for He cares for you. Be sober, be vigilant; because your adversary the devil walks about like a roaring lion, seeking whom he may devour. Resist him, steadfast in the faith..."

1 Peter 5:7-9

The term "casting," as used in 1 Peter, derives from the banking world meaning an exchange. It referred to a deposit that grew in interest where you would receive a greater return on your investment. When you allow the transformation process to exchange your strength for His, you learn to exercise your faith in His Word. He teaches you to focus on opportunities rather than obstacles.

Jesus promises to be with you during the trials and tribulations of this life. He gives you peace despite your circumstances. The believers in Philadelphia were few in number but were an army of faith. They drew strength from one another as they individually exercised their faith in Christ and His promises.

**TRANSFORMATIONAL TRUTH:
UNBELIEF SEES THE OBSTACLES; FAITH SEES THE OPPORTUNITIES.**

WHERE IS THE FOCUS OF YOUR FAITH TODAY? ARE YOU PLACING YOUR STRENGTH IN GOD AND HIS WORD? WHAT CARES DO YOU NEED TO CAST UPON HIM? THE HYMN "AMAZING GRACE" IS A RENOWNED TESTIMONY OF BELIEF AND GRATITUDE. WHILE MANY TAKE GREAT COMFORT FOR ITS FINAL VERSE, THE THIRD VERSE HAS BECOME MY FAVORITE THROUGH THE YEARS.

"THROUGH MANY DANGERS TOILS AND SNARES
I HAVE ALREADY COME.
TIS GRACE THAT BROUGHT ME SAVE THUS FAR,
AND GRACE WILL LEAD ME HOME."

Philadelphia was a large trade route of the Roman Empire, known as "the gateway to the East." From this city, God wanted to take a handful of faithful believers to touch the known world with the gospel. God saw not only what they were, but what they could become as they continued to submit their lives to His plan. Jesus told the believers of Philadelphia that He knew their works. He understands where you are in relation to His will for your life. He desires to bless you, lead you, and honor you. Your responsibility is to abide in Him. You must allow the Holy Spirit to flow through you to see His Kingdom advanced. Whether you are walking in fellowship with Him, or need to return to Him for restoration, His Word is the same for us all. He declares unchanging love for everyone and invites you to join Him again in the building of His Kingdom.

REFLECT

If God gave you a performance review or evaluation would He extend an offer to an open door?

Would God bring a word of commendation, or would His challenge be one of repentance?

In your sphere of influence, what doors are an invitation to impact His Kingdom?

DAY 3

AN INTIMATE INVITATION

"…you have not denied my Name…"

Revelation 3:8

The believers in Philadelphia, the city of brotherly love, would be honored and overwhelmed by the love of Jesus Christ. Their genuine devotion to Jesus would be distinguished from those who claimed to serve Him verbally but denied His Name when put to the test. When you use your strength to obey His Word and glorify His Name, Jesus says that your perseverance is recognized by your enemies. It is something the adversary cannot quench.

Followers of Christ lived in the midst of a pagan culture that embraced the gods of wine, women, and song. This culture would have looked the other way had the believers chosen to deny His Name. If confronted in these circumstances, would you deny or glorify His name? The believers in Philadelphia were presented with opportunities of denial, yet chose to remain faithful to the Name of Jesus. They regularly faced spiritual warfare from the "synagogue of Satan." Unbelievers would one day be compelled to worship before the faithful Philadelphian believers' feet. Opportunities came from those who claimed to represent God and yet were imposters. One thing is for certain, no matter the degree to which the Philadelphians faced persecution, they carried on. Their perseverance would result in a public affirmation that Jesus loves them. He opens doors that are kept locked or closed to the compromising believer.

TRANSFORMATIONAL TRUTH:
YOUR INTIMACY DETERMINES YOUR IMPACT.

INTIMACY WITH CHRIST OPENS THE DOOR THAT NO ONE, HUMAN OR DEMONIC, CAN CLOSE. THE INVITATION TO INTIMACY IS FOUND IN THE NATURE OF YOUR RELATIONSHIP WITH JESUS. HE INVITES YOU FIRST TO COME TO HIM, THEN TO FOLLOW HIM, AND FINALLY TO ABIDE IN HIM. IT IS YOUR ABIDING IN CHRIST THAT PRODUCES INTIMACY WHICH RESULTS IN OBEDIENCE. YOUR GOAL IS NOT TO TRY AND REPRESENT HIM AS IMPOSTERS DO, BUT TO KNOW HIM! IN KNOWING HIM YOU BRING GLORY AND HONOR TO HIS NAME.

Whether He is blessing me with prosperity or pruning me for future growth, the greatest challenge in my walk with Christ is to abide in Him. Resting in Him draws the focus to Christ, and not to myself. It is Christ in me that transforms my life into the image of Christ through the power of the Holy Spirit. Paul understood this in 2 Corinthians 3:18.

> *"But we all, with unveiled face, beholding as in a mirror the glory of the Lord, are being transformed into the same image from glory to glory, just as by the Spirit of the Lord."*

Jesus told the church of Philadelphia that He knew their good works. Do your works reflect the glory of Christ within, as you try to imitate intimacy with Him? When you stand at the Judgment Seat of Christ, the true impact of your intimacy will be realized as Christ rewards you for all of eternity.

I have used the simple phrase "You have all of God you want!" throughout my thirty years of pastoral ministry. The door to God is always open to those who choose to have an intimate relationship with Him. All the required ingredients for your spiritual transformation and intimacy with Christ have already been provided. He who has an ear, let him hear what the Spirit is saying to the churches.

REFLECT

Write down and meditate on the time in your life that you felt the closest to Jesus Christ.

Compare that to the time you felt the farthest from His presence. What brought you back to Him?

What step do you need to take to move closer to Christ?

DAY 4

OVERCOMING RELIGION

*"He who overcomes, I will make him a pillar
in the Temple of My God…"*

Revelation 3:12

The open door to the believers in Philadelphia not only resulted in a transformational process on Earth but also in Heaven. You may ask yourself, who is the "overcomer" that John is referring to in verse twelve? John addresses this as he writes to the believer for the purpose of fellowship and transformation. He reveals that believers and followers of Jesus Christ are the overcomers of the world.

*"For whatever is born of God overcomes the world.
And this is the victory that has overcome the world—
our faith. Who is he that overcomes the world, but he
who believes that Jesus is the Son of God."*

1 John 5:4-5

TRANSFORMATIONAL TRUTH: CHRISTIANITY IS ABOUT A RELATIONSHIP, NOT A RELIGION.

BEFORE YOU CAN CELEBRATE THE TRANSFORMA-
TIONAL TRUTHS THAT YOU WILL HAVE ON EARTH
AND IN ETERNITY, YOU MUST BE AN OVERCOMER.
YOU MUST HAVE A PERSONAL RELATIONSHIP WITH
JESUS CHRIST. YOU MUST HAVE A STORY OF HOW
YOU GAVE YOUR LIFE TO JESUS CHRIST BY FAITH AND
TRUST IN HIM.

I was raised in a home where my father knew about Jesus Christ but didn't know him personally as Lord and Savior. My father's biggest demon in life was a crippling alcohol addiction, so my mother was the spiritual hero of our family. Mom was a strong believer in Jesus Christ and she poured her faith into me, as well as my three older brothers. When I was a child, we attended church a lot. Sunday morning, our average worship service was almost three hours sitting on a wooden pew, which was pretty tough for an eight-year-old kid! We attended Sunday evenings, Monday evenings for a women's group called "willing workers," Wednesday evenings for youth and children's night, and Saturday evenings for a prayer service. From my earliest childhood memory, we held family devotions in our home every day of every year. We would act out the Bible stories, sing the great hymns, and memorize scriptures. Naturally, the church became a part of our spiritual DNA.

August of 1964, we went to church same as every Sunday. How was I to know that this particular morning would change my life forever? My mother played the piano, the guitar, and had a beautiful alto voice. She would use her spiritual giftedness to lead in the worship service. This service, our guest speaker was an officer in the military and a survivor of the Bataan death march in the Philippines. When I was a kid, we would play with toy army men and set up battlefield scenarios. So, when he began telling World War II stories, he had my complete attention. When the evangelist came to a conclusion in his message, he asked Mom to come play the piano as he gave an invitation. I watched as Mom arose and began to walk away from me. It was in that moment that the Holy Spirit spoke to an eight-year-old child and said, your Mother is going somewhere you're not going!

I realized that you don't go to Heaven because you attend the church five times per week, read the Bible in your home, and memorize scriptures. I had to make a personal decision about this Man called Jesus. I took about three to five steps towards the evangelist and took his hand. He asked me a simple question, "Why did you come forward?" I wanted to receive Jesus Christ as my personal Lord and Savior. If he would have asked me about soteriology, pneumatology, hamartiology, or eschatology, I wouldn't have a clue how to respond. What I knew was this, Heaven is real; Hell is hot; Jesus saves. It was at that moment my eternal destiny was sealed forever.

Christ has opened the door to believers, just as he did with His followers in Philadelphia. Once you accept Jesus as the Son of God, the open door welcomes you to be a part of an eternal family. Whether you are eight or eighty, give your life to Jesus today and you will become part of the Family of God.

REFLECT

What or who are you trusting to get you off of Earth and into Heaven one day?

Do you have a personal relationship with Jesus Christ that you can clearly articulate?

If you have never received Jesus as your Personal Savior, I want you to pray this with me...

Dear Father,

Today I ask You to forgive me of my sins. By faith, I ask You Jesus to be my Lord and Savior. Thank You for Your free gift of salvation through a relationship with Jesus Christ. Amen.

Welcome to the Family!

DAY 5

WINNING THE WAR

"Behold, I am coming quickly..."

Revelation 3:11

Surrendering your life to Jesus is the greatest single decision you will ever make. If you're still pondering this decision, I encourage you to stop waiting and give your life to Jesus. He is coming, and there must be a sense of urgency in your life regarding this choice. If Christ comes and the trumpet sounds to call His church home today, you will be left behind. Time is a commodity that you cannot waste when it comes to your salvation.

**TRANSFORMATIONAL TRUTH:
I MAY LOSE A BATTLE NOW AND THEN,
BUT I'VE ALREADY WON THE WAR!**

YOU CAN REST IN CHRIST KNOWING HE HAS PROMISED THAT THE HOLY SPIRIT WILL NEVER LEAVE NOR FORSAKE YOU. THE BELIEVERS AT PHILADELPHIA HAD LITTLE STRENGTH. THEY HADN'T WON EVERY BATTLE, BUT THEY REMAINED FAITHFUL TO TRUST HIS WORD AND NOT DENY HIS NAME. THIS GRANTED THE CHURCH OF PHILADELPHIA AN INVITATION TO IMPACT THE KINGDOM THROUGH THE OPEN DOOR. JESUS GIVES THE SAME INVITATION TO BELIEVERS TODAY WHO HAVE A PERSONAL, GROWING, AND ABIDING WALK WITH THE HOLY SPIRIT.

If you are a believer in Jesus Christ and have a personal relationship with Him, you are an overcomer. The One who is holy, who is true, and who holds the keys to death, Hell, and the grave is now your Lord! When Jesus returns, He promises to reward you with the following expressions of eternal recognition.

1) He will make you a pillar in the temple of My God as a part of your eternal transformation. In Biblical times, a pillar would be carved out to preserve the history of a city or nation and honor those who made an impact in the culture. The pillars contained records that were sealed inside to prevent any conquering enemy from burning the heritage of their nation. A pillar speaks of how Jesus recognizes and honors you in eternity as an overcomer. 2) He will

write upon you the Name of His God and speak to the principle of ownership. Jesus purchased you and me off of the slave market of sin and we become His servants. 3) He will give you access to the city of Jerusalem forever and speaks to your eternal security in Christ. 4) He will give you the right to His Name and the fullness and privileges it brings. You are adopted into His family for all of eternity.

All of these privileges of honor and recognition are yours by faith in Jesus Christ. On Earth, you are being transformed into the image of God's Son. In Heaven, you are eternally the bearer of His image. Your intimacy with Christ, abiding in His presence on Earth, grants you access to all the acknowledgment in eternity. You need to be earnest in your life to remain filled with the Holy Spirit and live as an overcomer.

REFLECT

What areas of your life has the enemy been holding you hostage that you need to release to Christ today?

Have you asked Christ to forgive you for the battles lost and to give you confidence to serve Him in the future?

In what ways has the Holy Spirit spoken to your heart? Will you allow the Holy Spirit to cleanse you and recommission you for His serve today?

II

THE DOORS OF SALVATION

John 10:7-17

The "I Am" statements found in the Gospel of John introduce the deity of God's Son, Jesus Christ. Jesus used the metaphor of a door to describe His analogy of the good shepherd to His sheep. Those who walk through this door are under the care of the *eternal* shepherd and provider.

In this passage, Jesus describes Himself as *the* door. The emphasis of *the* as a definitive article brings great clarity to what Jesus describes. He is the only door that will provide for eternity. Not only will He guide, protect, feed, correct, comfort, and nurture in time, but He alone provides for the security of His sheep for all of eternity. You must choose to walk through this door that leads to an abundant life.

DAY 6

I AM...

"I am the Door..."

John 10:9

John 10 includes one of seven metaphors used by Jesus to shock the people. It states that Jesus Christ was the good shepherd, who alone could lead His sheep through the door of salvation. The "I Am" statements express God's desire to show all of mankind that Christianity is not about religion, but about a relationship. He is a sovereign, self-existing God known by the Jewish nation as the "I Am that I Am." I am the bread of life. I am the light of the world. I am the resurrection. I am the way, the truth, and the life. All of these declarative statements distinguished Jesus from all other messages they received. He was the authentic, genuine, unique, separate, and eternal "I Am" who wasn't a distant deity, but a Shepherd who would give His life for His sheep.

Israel met many others who claimed to be their deliverer. These pretenders proclaimed to be the conquering king, sent to deliver the Jewish nation from their current bondage under the oppression of the Roman Empire. God's plan, since the Garden of Eden, was to send a Savior who could reconcile man with God and restore the relationship broken when mankind sinned. Before there could be a king crowned, a Savior had to be sacrificed to pay the redemptive price set by God Himself. Only Jesus claimed to be their Shepherd. He alone claimed to be their God. God the Father had sent God the Son to die for the sins of the world.

The Old Testament gave unmistakable signs that the good Shepherd had come to give His life for His sheep (John 10:11). The reality of God's Son could be proven by the works that He did (John 10:25). Jesus would have power over nature (John 6:15-21), sin (John 1:29), disease (John 4:46-54; John Chapter 9), demons (Luke 9:1; Mark Chapter 5), and death (John 11:25-26).

The ultimate reality would be His death, burial, and resurrection (John 10:17-18). This man called Jesus is the only Son of the only living God. The reality of John 10 is that in one "I Am" statement, Jesus proclaimed that He existed for all eternity. He alone is God's Son sent to seek and to save that which was lost. Jesus claimed to be the everlasting and self-existent God!

TRANSFORMATIONAL TRUTH:
JESUS DIDN'T COME TO MAKE EARTHLY
ADJUSTMENTS, BUT ETERNAL ALTERATIONS!

NO ETERNAL CHANGE, NO CHRIST. ONE THIEF THAT HUNG BESIDE JESUS ON THE CROSS WAS LOOKING FOR AN EARTHLY ADJUSTMENT. HE SAID TO JESUS THAT IF HE WAS THE SON OF GOD, HE SHOULD COME OFF THE CROSS AND SAVE THEM. THIS THIEF WANTED HIS CIRCUMSTANCES CHANGED ON EARTH. THE SECOND THIEF SAW PAST THE EARTHLY AND TEMPORAL TO THE ETERNAL. HE REALIZED THAT JESUS WAS INNOCENT OF HIS ACCUSATIONS BUT GUILTY OF HIS ASSIGNMENT. HE WAS GOD'S SON WHO CAME TO DIE SO THAT YOU COULD BE RESTORED WITH GOD, NOT JUST FOR A TIME, BUT FOR ETERNITY. THE SAVIOR WHO WAS BEING SACRIFICED WAS THE KING ABOUT TO BE CROWNED! LORD, REMEMBER ME, WHEN I COME INTO YOUR KINGDOM.

Jesus said that as the good shepherd, He would lay down His life for His sheep. One day soon He will call His sheep who will not only hear His voice but will know His voice. Jesus will soon lead you through the door of Heaven to eternal safety. No change, no Christ! He has come to give you life and ensure that you have life more abundantly. Jesus is the only door to your salvation, and He is waiting for you to enter.

"After these things I looked and behold a door was opened in Heaven…"

Revelation 4:1

REFLECT

The door of salvation is the most important door you will ever walk through. What was the reality of your life before you found Christ?

The door of salvation focuses on your personal relationship with Jesus Christ. How did you find Jesus Christ as your Lord and Savior?

The door of salvation focuses on the reality that your encounter with Christ has changed your life. How has your life changed since coming to Christ?

DAY 7

A SEALED TOMB

"And behold, there was a great earthquake; for an angel of the Lord descended from heaven, and came and rolled back the stone from the door, and sat on it."

Matthew 28:2

The disciples of Jesus' week began with a triumphal entry into Jerusalem, only to see Jesus dismount the donkey He traveled by and weep uncontrollably on the ground. The people surrounded Jesus to honor Him with praise and quote the Word. They were lining the road with their coats and branches from the palm tree. Those who sought a deliverer sprinkled the dusty road to Jerusalem with their tears. He was someone who would lift the oppression of the Roman Empire. The people would finally be free from the Roman Eagle hanging over the gates of Jerusalem.

However, this triumph turned into betrayal. The celebration in the streets was followed with Jesus' arrest and ended at a crucifix. The disciples gathered into the Upper Room to celebrate The Passover Meal where Jesus affirmed His death again. He shocked His followers by humbly washing their feet as a mere servant before them. He spoke to them about His broken body and His shed blood, as a memorial to Himself. They left singing a hymn together as Jesus prepared for His hour of decision. When they arrived at the Garden of Gethsemane, Jesus invited them to pray. The prayers became so intense that Jesus began to sweat drops of blood, even as the betrayer approached the Garden. Before man ever took a drop of His blood, Jesus had already shed it for you. A kiss on the cheek led to a violent confrontation as Peter tried to stop Jesus' hour from ending. Jesus takes a severed ear from the ground and reattaches it as if nothing had ever happened. In His last hours on Earth, Jesus performed a miracle only a Messiah could accomplish.

When the trials began, the mocking, scourging, denials, and betrayals all led to Via Dolorosa, the road to Calvary. The Romans drove nails through His hands and feet. In mockery, they placed a sign over His head that read, "This is the King of the Jews."

**TRANSFORMATIONAL TRUTH:
THE HUMAN, THE DIVINE, AND THE DEMONIC
ALL WOULD HAVE THEIR PLACE AT THE CROSS.**

AT DEATH, THESE THREE BEINGS ARE ALWAYS INVOLVED. BEFORE THE DOOR OF STONE CAN BE ROLLED AWAY FROM YOUR LIFE, A DEATH HAD TO OCCUR. LIFE CANNOT BE RECEIVED WITHOUT A SACRIFICIAL DEATH. JESUS DIED SO YOU COULD

LIVE; YOU DIE TO SELF SO YOU CAN LIVE. LET YOUR
SELFISHNESS, TEMPTATIONS, AND WORLDLY DESIRES
DEPART AS YOU GIVE YOUR LIFE TO JESUS. ALLOW
CHRIST TO LEAD YOUR LIFE.

The human has its place as we go through the valley of the shadow of death. The valley of the shadow of death is a real place between Jerusalem and Jericho, in which there are places that the sun never shines. At Calvary, the sun refused to shine as Jesus became sin for you and me. The Divine blotted out the sun for three hours as God's Son was bearing our sin on the cross. The Father and the Holy Spirit had forsaken the Son. Jesus had been made into a sin offering. The demonic world rejoiced over His sufferings and His death, as the sting of death stung the humanity of Jesus Christ. His final cry, "It is finished," led to a borrowed tomb and a door of stone. No hinges to swing open. No lock to which there was a key. No window into the tomb. Only a door of stone.

> *"When Joseph had taken the body, he wrapped it in a clean linen cloth, and laid it in his new tomb which he had hewn out of the rock; and he rolled a large stone against the door of the tomb, and departed."*

> *Matthew 27:59-60*

REFLECT

Have you ever come face to face with a door of stone? There is no window, no key, and no hope. When you face a door of stone, you need divine help. Have you asked for His help?

Are you still seeking a human answer for a divine problem? Sometimes the only answer to human impossibility is to admit it is humanly impossible! A door of stone can become a door of possibility when we give it to Jesus.

Jesus is the only one that can open the door of stone to your heart and set you free. Have you asked Jesus to be your Savior and Lord? If not, do so now.

"That if you confess with your mouth the Lord Jesus and believe in your heart that God raised Him from the dead, you will be saved. For with the heart one believes unto righteousness and with the mouth confession is made unto salvation."

Romans 10:9-10

DAY 8

THERE'S ALWAYS TOMORROW

"On the next day..."

Matthew 27:62

Joseph, Nicodemus, and their servants rolled a large stone against the door of Jesus' tomb before departing. Both of these men encountered Jesus Christ, but neither had taken a public stand for Him. Imagine for a moment that Joseph is standing outside the Praetorium. Watch as he pauses, takes a deep breath, and walks before Pilate to identify Himself with Jesus Christ! Both of these men (Joseph and Nicodemus) were in hiding at the end of Jesus' life, but they went public when He died. The disciples who went public during Jesus' life went into hiding at His death.

**TRANSFORMATIONAL TRUTH:
THERE IS ALWAYS A NEXT DAY WITH JESUS.**

"ON THE NEXT DAY," IMPLIES THAT THE STORY IS STILL BEING WRITTEN. THE STONE WASN'T A PERIOD, IT WAS AN EXCLAMATION POINT TO ALL THAT THE WORLD COULD DO TO JESUS! THE PROBLEM WITH JESUS IS THAT HE WAS CRUCIFIED AND BRUTALLY KILLED ON FRIDAY, BUT YOU BUMP INTO HIM ON THE STREETS OF JERUSALEM ON SUNDAY. NEVER FORGET THAT NO MATTER WHAT HAS HAPPENED IN YOUR LIFE, YOUR STORY IS STILL BEING WRITTEN. THERE IS ALWAYS A NEXT DAY WITH JESUS!

"So they went and made the tomb secure, sealing the stone and setting the guard."

Matthew 27:66

The chief priests and Pharisees also had a next day experience with Jesus. They remembered that Jesus had made an outrageous claim to be God and that He would prove it by rising from the dead after the third day. They too approached Pilate requesting something surrounding Jesus, the King of the Jews, whom they had crucified. They came up with a conspiracy theory in addition to an earthly solution. They would seal the tomb, secure the tomb with special forces, and send a clear message to any other so-called Messiah that this would be their fate. Let this stone door be a sign and symbol to all who would oppose their authority and the authority of Rome.

The empty tomb is the enduring symbol and ultimate representation of Jesus' claim to being God. The resurrection of Jesus Christ changes everything, even the calendar you look at every day! The cross reminds you of His brutal death. The empty tomb reminds you of new beginnings. Rome had spoken; Religion had spoken; the realm of the supernatural had spoken. Death, decay, darkness, and demons had spoken with one word of acclamation: Defeated. It was now God's turn to show up. Isn't it time you gave your life to Christ?

REFLECT

If you don't believe that Jesus died, was buried, and rose again on the third day have you examined the evidence for yourself?

Are you willing to stake your opinion on the resurrection of Jesus Christ solely based on the opinion of someone else?

What is one example of a next day experience with Jesus Christ when you were facing a stone door of impossibility and Jesus rolled the stone away? Share this experience with someone today.

DAY 9

SEAT OF STONE

*"...for an angel of the Lord descended from heaven, came and rolled back the stone from the door, **and sat on it**."*

Matthew 28:2

Inside the door of stone, lies the results of a hill called Calvary. The darkness of Calvary led to the eclipse of the sealed tomb. The death that occurred in public now finds isolation and defeat. Religion and Rome had now spoken, and for three days despair had reigned. No one on Earth dared to question the authority of Rome. The men who were ordered to guard the tomb certainly didn't expect anything to happen, as one guard could defend and defeat up to ten men himself. What a degrading, laughable assignment. They had mocked Jesus the king of the Jews during His death and were now assigned to make sure He stayed dead.

The religious leaders knew of Jesus' claim to rise again on the third day, and the clock had been ticking.

It seemed inconceivable to the religious leaders, yet they remembered His boisterous claim of the sign of Jonah. As Jonah was in the belly of the whale three days so Jesus would be, and He would rise again. They wanted to make sure that this self-proclaimed Messiah, whose works and miracles they could not deny, would stay dead. The religious leaders sought out Rome's best men to protect the tomb. No one would be able to get through these guards, and no one would be able to roll the door of stone away! They were confident that this would be the end.

No one in Jerusalem would dare question the authority of the religious leaders, or they would risk being labeled ceremonially unclean and a religious outcast. Long gone were the waving of palm branches and the ceremonial laying of the robes as a sign of triumphant worship. The cheers of "Hosanna" had been replaced with the cry "crucify Him" as they blamed another failed Messiah for their bondage in this life. No one was sent to the tomb to report the story. Dead is dead and buried is buried.

The Christ-followers were briefed on several occasions, informing them that Jesus would indeed rise from the dead. Jesus taught that He was to be made sin for the sins of the world. He must be first a suffering Savior (Isaiah 53) before He could be their conquering King. The disciples and followers of Jesus all went into hiding as they knew someone would ask, "Aren't you one of those Christ-followers?" just as they had questioned Peter. Hiding was their only solution. They had witnessed the betrayal, arrest, scourging's, mock trials, and crucifixion. Somewhere during that process, all of them made their exits.

The women approached the tomb expecting to find the dead body of Jesus. They pondered how they would be able to get past the stone door to ceremonially anoint Jesus' body. Although it would be a challenge, they still came to attempt the task. Perhaps they would receive compassion from the guards, or maybe the gardener would provide an answer. No matter what would happen, they still came by faith.

TRANSFORMATIONAL TRUTH:
WHEN FAITH SHOWS UP, DOORS OF STONE GET OPENED.

THE CROSS BECAME THE PLATFORM FOR HIS THRONE. THIS QUALIFIED JESUS TO ENTER PARADISE AS THE SACRIFICIAL LAMB OF GOD AND RETURN AS THE GOD-MAN IN A RESURRECTED BODY. THE ANGEL CAME AND ROLLED THE STONE AWAY AS A SIGN OF TRIUMPH OVER DEATH, HELL, THE GRAVE, RELIGION, ROME, AND DOUBT. THE ANGEL TRIUMPHANTLY AND MOCKINGLY SAT ON THE STONE. WHEN DOORS OF STONE ARE REMOVED, GOD'S WORK IS DONE AND TO BE SEATED IS THE ABSOLUTE VICTORY. THERE IS NO MORE FEAR OF ATTACK FROM THE HUMAN, RELIGIOUS, NOR SUPERNATURAL REALM. THE DOOR OF STONE WILL NOT BE REPLACED AND THE TOMB IS FOREVER EMPTY! JESUS WANTS TO NOT ONLY DELIVER YOU FROM DARKNESS, DEFEAT, DECAY, AND DOUBT, BUT HE WANTS TO GIVE YOU LIFE MORE ABUNDANTLY.

"The thief does not come except to kill, steal, and destroy. I have come that they may have life, and that they may have it more abundantly."

John 10:10

REFLECT

What doors of stone are you facing right now that only Jesus can move?

When faith shows up, even a mustard seed of faith, God will move mountains. Mountains of guilt disintegrate. Mountains of defeat are banished. Mountains of dreams begin to receive new life. Are you willing to trust that He can triumph over your personal tragedy and disappointment?

Stone doors keep you in the tombs of depression, despair, and denial. Seek help because it takes heavy equipment to move doors of stone. How can you start the process of stone removal today?

"Therefore humble yourselves under the mighty hand of God, that He may exalt you in due time, casting all your cares upon Him, for He cares for you!"

1 Peter 5:6-7

III

THE DOORS OF FELLOWSHIP

Revelation 3:20

The door of fellowship is a passionate view of how much Jesus desires to spend time with you. The God who knows all about you, searches and pursues you, even when you walk away from His plan for your life. Jesus is calling out your name and knocking on the door of your heart.

The door of fellowship is a door of hope. It's an invitation to a new beginning, a new way of thinking about our Lord and Savior. Jesus isn't mad at you and is never avoiding you. He wants to have dinner with you! The King of kings desires to spend time with you. Let this door give you encouragement, joy, and above all, hope!

DAY 10

FORE!

"Behold, I stand at the door at knock. If anyone hears My voice and opens the door, I will come in to him and dine with him, and he with Me."

Revelation 3:20

In golf, we yell "fore" if we need to get someone's attention quickly when an errant shot is heading their way. This exclamation warns a golfer to take immediate action by either covering his head or attempting to hide behind his golf cart. No one in the golfing world questions this yell, we only look to see from what direction the cry came. One good thing that comes from hearing that shout is when the shot actually misses the golfer. When I hear the word "fore" on the golf course, it makes the hair on the back of my neck stand up. Having been struck by a golf ball, I can promise you I take that call very seriously!

Behold. The word doesn't mean much to the generation in which we live, but first century Christianity knew exactly what the term meant. It is a word designed to get your undivided attention carrying both a positive and a negative effect. In Revelation 1:7, the word behold announced the reality of the second coming of Jesus Christ and the judgment associated with it. In Revelation 1:18, behold declares the risen Savior being alive forevermore, and possesses the keys to death, Hell, and the grave. Revelation 4:1 uses behold in the context that the church will be raptured to Heaven and ushered into the very throne room of God.

**TRANSFORMATIONAL TRUTH:
JESUS IS KNOCKING AT YOUR DOOR;
HE WANTS YOUR ATTENTION.**

WHAT DOES IT TAKE TO GET YOUR ATTENTION? DOES IT TAKE A LIFE-ALTERING MOMENT? A PRODIGAL, A PHONE CALL, A ROUTINE PHYSICAL PROCEDURE, OR A PORTFOLIO THAT IS GONE IN A MOMENT? JESUS BEGINS WITH A KNOCK ON YOUR DOOR, TRYING TO BREAK INTO THE ROUTINE OF YOUR LIFE AND OFFER MORE OF HIMSELF. SIMPLY PUT, BEHOLD IS AN EXCLAMATION AND IS ALWAYS USED IN A DRAMATIC SENSE. JESUS STANDS OUTSIDE TO KNOCK ON THE FRONT DOOR OF YOUR LIFE. THIS INVITATION WILL CHANGE YOU FOREVER. THE INVITATION IS FOR MORE OF CHRIST; A PRIVATE LUNCHEON WITH THE KING OF KINGS AND THE LORD OF LORDS.

The imagery Jesus uses is striking. The risen, omnipotent, Savior of the world is standing outside on the front porch. He knocks not only on the door of the church but the door of the individual members of the body of Christ. Your volition is emphasized by the knocking of Jesus Christ and His longing for someone to open the door. You must choose to open the door and invite Christ into your home to have fellowship with Him.

Think of the repercussions for not answering the door. The loss of fellowship with Christ. The forfeiture of spiritual blessings for yourself, your family, and your friends. The undue stress that continues to build. The lack of intimacy in your relationship with Christ. You would have nothing but a superfluous, surface relationship that lacks growth with Him. Life in Christ is characterized by anxiety, frustration, and a God that will become boring if you keep your door shut.

Think of what happens when you hear a knock on the door and choose to answer, only to find that the King of kings is hungry to have a deeper relationship with you. It's not about what you can do for Him. There is no list of what you need to do for a deeper relationship with Jesus. He just wants you, to want Him, as much as He wants you! He wants to see the smile He brings to your face when you open the door. You receive the joy of knowing that He loves you and isn't too busy for you. The fragrance of peace saturates the room. His words are refreshing as you hear His voice call you by name. The voice that calmed and controlled the sea now calms and controls your life. Eternity replaces time.

"More of you, more of you, I've had all but what I need is more of you. Of things I've had my fill and

yet I hunger still, empty and bare, Lord hear my prayer for more of you."

More of You - Gaither Vocal Band

REFLECT

The "behold" moment is a knocking that never ceases as Jesus pursues after you for an intimate relationship with Him. Take a moment to bow your head and listen as He knocks.

What will it take to get your undivided attention? Do you realize He loves you so much that He'll keep knocking?

The invitation of unbroken fellowship is given to His bride, the church, for whom He died. If you've never said yes to Jesus as Savior, will you open the door of your heart today?

DAY 11

A DIVINE COLD CALL

"Behold, I stand at the door and knock. If anyone hears My voice and opens the door, I will come in to him and dine with him, and he with Me."

Revelation 3:20

The position of Jesus Christ in this passage is one of great significance. The last time Jesus is seen standing is at the death of Stephen in Acts 7:55-56. As Stephen is being stoned to death, he sees the heavens open where Jesus stands at the right hand of God. Since Jesus' resurrection and ascension, He is seen as the eternal High Priest. He is seated at the right hand of God who ever lives to make intercession for His bride, the church. Jesus stands, displaying a position of tribute and honor to His servant Stephen as he is being martyred for the name of his Lord and Savior.

In the last message to the church (Revelation 3:20) Jesus is knocking on the door, asking to be let in. The church is composed of individual members of the body of Jesus Christ. You and I are the body of Christ, the church. As such, Jesus desires to have an unbroken fellowship with us as individuals. The church at Laodicea had grown independent of Jesus Christ and had become dependent upon themselves. Jesus describes self-evaluation, without total dependence on Jesus Christ, as wretched, miserable, poor, blind, and naked. In our terminology, these people would live as dejected, pitied beggars.

TRANSFORMATIONAL TRUTH: IF YOU OPEN YOUR DOOR, JESUS WILL BE STANDING OUTSIDE.

SUPPOSE YOU HEARD THE KNOCK ON YOUR DOOR AND YOU LOOKED OUT THE PEEPHOLE TO FIND JESUS STANDING OUTSIDE. WHAT WOULD YOUR RESPONSE BE? WHEN YOU FEEL LIKE YOU DON'T NEED HIM AS THE CENTER OF YOUR LIFE, YOU'LL LEAVE HIM STANDING OUTSIDE. JESUS LOVES YOU AND ME SO MUCH THAT HE CHANGED POSITIONS FROM SITTING TO STANDING ON YOUR BEHALF. YOU WOULD LIKE TO SAY THAT YOU'D NEVER IGNORE THE DOOR KNOCK, BUT IN REALITY, YOU DO IT EACH DAY YOU FAIL TO SPEND IN FELLOWSHIP WITH HIM.

I used to work sales back in the seventies and made cold calls to homes. Back then, people weren't as cold as they are today. No one knew I was coming and from their responses, they weren't interested in what I had to sell. It was difficult being rejected time and time again, but most people were at least courteous enough to answer the door. The most difficult calls were when I could hear televisions playing, people talking, and dogs barking loud enough to wake the dead, yet the door was simply ignored. As I stood there, I would have loved to have been able to say to folks, "If you only knew how bad I need this sale to feed my family you'd hopefully have sympathy and open the door."

I cannot begin to fathom how Christ feels when we ignore His knocking. He died for us, promised to never leave nor forsake us, and yet we live our lives as if we don't need Him. He shared that He is the vine and we are the branches. Without Him, we can do nothing. What we work for to attain in this life adds up to nothing without Christ. What we call success, He calls nothing. What we take pride in, He calls nothing. He stands diligently at the door and keeps knocking on our hearts. The blessings and benefits of opening the door are beyond description.

He doesn't do this to make you feel guilty, although we all are. Be grateful for a Savior who always pursues you even when you rebel and reject His advances. In spite of your guilt, He offers more grace. The more that you ignore Him, the louder He knocks. May you see the grace that lies on the other side of the closed door in front of you. Run into His arms.

REFLECT

If you feel unworthy to open the door, ask yourself why He keeps knocking. He sees you as His child of infinite, eternal worth and value. Open the door and run into His arms.

Have you ever been stood up? You had an agreed time to meet, a date and location were set and then you realized that the person was a "no show." Jesus will always show up. He's never late; He's always on time.

Jesus' persistence after you is a sign that you're genuinely loved and are His child. Allow His grace to overwhelm you with His presence today!

DAY 12

AT THE DOOR

"Behold, I stand at the door and knock. If anyone hears My voice and opens the door, I will come in to him and dine with him, and he with Me."

Revelation 3:20

I'll never forget the first time I was "shown" the door. The slang term means to be asked to leave the room or, in my case, the house. I was invited to an individual's home to answer questions about my faith and what our church's belief was on a specific subject. Once I arrived, and after answering numerous questions, I realized that we were not even on the same planet regarding our answers. No matter what I said or how hard I tried to diffuse the situation, we were heading towards disaster. Our answers didn't determine the eternal impact of Heaven or Hell, but they were unquestionably on opposite ends of the spectrum. I could tell the gentlemen was getting quite agitated, as he believed this topic was a grey area in the scriptures. So, I was "shown" out the door of a home that I was invited to enter.

The door was opened in a very gentle manner when I arrived but was closed with a definitive thud when ushered out. I've learned that I'm capable of doing the same thing spiritually speaking when I feel pressed by the Lord. Especially when He asks me to follow a plan that does not align with my own. I don't show Him the door but instead, stop talking to Him. I decide not to live in fellowship with Him because, for some moment of temporary insanity, I think I know what's best for my life. It's in moments like this that Jesus is standing outside of the room I'm occupying, knocking on the door, waiting for it to open.

Doors are designed by construction to provide a barrier between the inside and outside. They keep out the elements of cold, rain, sleet, snow, and wind. Providing a barrier of security and protection against unwanted guests or intruders. Jesus shows up unannounced and knocks. He doesn't tire or is ever in need of a chair. He stands and knocks, waiting for you.

**TRANSFORMATIONAL TRUTH:
JESUS IS KNOCK, KNOCK, KNOCKING
ON YOUR DOOR.**

BOB DYLAN WROTE A FAMOUS SONG WITH THE LYRICS "KNOCK, KNOCK, KNOCKING ON HEAVEN'S DOOR." ANOTHER SONG SAYS, "TWO DOORS DOWN THEY'RE LAUGHING AND DRINKING AND HAVING A PARTY, TWO DOORS DOWN THEIR NOT AWARE THAT I'M AROUND." AS JESUS STANDS AND KNOCKS

ON YOUR DOOR, YOU MAY THINK HE IS MISTAKEN, BUT HE DOESN'T HAVE THE WRONG DOOR. HE'S AWARE THAT YOU'RE AROUND AND THAT HE WANTS TO SPEND TIME WITH YOU TODAY. IF NOT TODAY, HE'LL KEEP KNOCKING! HE DESIRES TO BE WITH YOU MORE THAN YOU COULD EVER IMAGINE.

Jesus will keep knocking because He wants to demonstrate His unconditional love for you. I may not feel worthy to open the door and invite Him into my home. I may not want to face the music for the decisions I've made. He continues to stand and knock. With persistent patience and concern, He demonstrates His faithfulness to me by not walking away to leave me on my own.

In 1981, I made a personal decision to walk out of the church and not return. I had taken my eyes of Christ and placed them on people. I believed that "If this is church, who needs it?" For the next five years, I didn't go to any church. My heart became harder and harder. I continued to read my Bible, pray over food at mealtime, and do an occasional devotion, but I was miserable. During my prodigal journey of almost five years, Jesus Christ never left the door and never ceased to knock. He will always have unconditional love for His church, the bride of Christ.

REFLECT

Does your front door have a welcome mat? Make sure that Jesus is welcome even if He shows up unannounced.

Does your front door have a peephole? Sometimes that's all the amount of faith you have. Take this moment to get a fresh glimpse of the Savior as He knocks on the door of your heart.

Have you ever been "shown" the door by anyone? Remember that feeling of rejection as you hear His knocking on your door.

DAY 13

THE POTENTIAL OF IF

"…If anyone…"

Revelation 3:20

Understanding language is imperative to the truth meant behind a statement. "If" is such a word. In the English language "if" is generally a subjunctive or implies a possibility. In the Greek language, this is not always the case. "If" in Revelation 3:20 represents the potential that lies within you to make a choice. You can answer the knocking at the door and invite Christ into your home, or you can choose to lock it and hide the key.

"If only," is a phrase commonly associated with regret. You look back at how your life might have been different if only you had made a different decision. If only you had picked up the phone and dialed the number. If only you hadn't gotten injured. What could have been if only you had acted sooner? The "if only" statements of life usually involve disappointment, indecisions, or pain. These statements have a paralyzing effect. They reflect the moments of your life when you were too passive or hesitated with your decisions.

The image of Jesus repeatedly knocking on an unanswered door urges you to take action. Those who have opened the door know of the joy and freedom on the other side. Lives will be changed and impacted for eternity. You understand the sphere of influence that each life possesses. You see the ripple effect of one intentional step towards that door. When you take the first step towards the door and open it to Christ, it's as if you are floating on air. There is a release in the human spirit as you allow Christ to enter.

I decided to walk away from Christ at age twenty-five. I had been hurt by Christian people. I took my eyes off of Jesus Christ and placed them upon my critics. Tragically, I looked at myself and thought that I deserved better. If only the critic could understand the hours my wife and I had given to others. If only they could see how we helped to change lives and ease the pain of others. If only they could have known the burden I felt to oversee teenagers passionately serving Christ. It's amazing how quickly "if only" can turn to an "I'm done" statement. Then the knocking begins. At first, it is so light that you can't hear it through your pain, anger, and bitterness. What once seemed like open doors to you now feels closed shut.

Jesus sees the potential within you to open the door again. His faithfulness means that He will persistently keep knocking. I can remember when I took the first step towards opening the door. I had been consistently brushing away my wife's request to attend church again.

It had been five years of knocking, followed by nearly five years of excuses. Years of ignoring and indifference suddenly hit home with the repercussions. My nine-year-old daughter asked if she could stay home from church with me.

**TRANSFORMATIONAL TRUTH:
JESUS WILL COME FOR YOUR HEART.**

JESUS WAS NOW POUNDING ON THE DOOR! HIS LOVE FORCED ME TO TAKE A RATHER BLUNT LOOK AT HOW I WAS INFLUENCING MY NINE-YEAR-OLD. SHE WANTED TO STAY HOME WITH HER DAD INSTEAD OF GOING TO CHURCH. WHEN JESUS BEGINS TO POUND ON THE DOOR, HE GOES STRAIGHT TO THE HEART.

After a very long pause, I explained to my daughter that I would be attending church with them that evening. My wife was so stunned that I thought we would have to call 911 to revive her. We loaded the car to head to the church, but there was a lot of built up defiance inside of me. I proceeded to tell my wife what I would not be participating in any church activities. I would never again sing with my wife. I would never work with teens or teach a bible study. I would go, but that would be the extent of my involvement. Somehow the pounding at the door in my mind began to ease to a tolerable level.

One Sunday evening, the service was about to come to a close when the pastor announced that they were going to have a baptism. I can remember thinking that I hadn't seen a baptism for quite a while, especially since I scheduled myself to work every Sunday morning. I can also remember trying to laugh away the moment by listening to the congregation sing, "Shall we gather at the river," and then watch a baptism in a hot tub. I wasn't ready for what happened next. As the pastor came down into the water, he invited a little seven-year-old boy to join him. As he came down the steps of the baptistery, Jesus was pounding at the door so loudly and clearly that I couldn't speak. All I could do was cry. I quickly stepped out of the pew and made my way to an altar. I knelt and opened the door! If only I had opened that door sooner, I would not feel as if I wasted away those five precious years of my life.

REFLECT

The invitation to answer the knocking extends to you today. Is there any good reason why you cannot open the door?

Do you have your eyes on everything and everyone other than Jesus?

What are you willing to sacrifice before you will open the door?

DAY 14

AN ALL-INCLUSIVE INVITATION

"If anyone…"

Revelation 3:20

"Anyone" is an all-inclusive invitation. It doesn't matter if you're male or female. It makes no difference what socio-economic standing you have. It invites and includes every ethnicity on the planet. It knows no boundaries, limitations, requirements, and requires no degrees. Anyone, is a word free from prejudice.

In Revelation chapter one, John sees Jesus in all His majesty at the Second Coming. John's vision gives a detailed description of His hair, eyes, clothing, belt, shoes, and voice. Jesus is standing in the center encircled by the seven churches to which John is to send this letter. He is at His rightful place as the center and head of the church for which He died. John goes on in chapters two and three to write brief letters to seven very different churches. Five of the churches will have some form of condemnation and rebuke. One church is to suffer for His namesake. The last church will be given an open door of influence and opportunity. The pastors of the churches, referred to as angels (messengers), are to be held in His hands.

TRANSFORMATIONAL TRUTH: JESUS ALREADY HAS YOUR RESUME.

EVERY DETAIL OF YOUR LIFE, BOTH GOOD AND BAD, POSITIVE AND NEGATIVE, ARE A PART OF YOUR RESUME. WHEN I WAS A CHILD GROWING UP, WE WOULD WATCH A SHOW CALLED "DRAGNET" WITH SERGEANT JOE FRIDAY. JOE FRIDAY'S CHARACTER HAD ONE LINE THAT BECAME A HOUSEHOLD FAVORITE. EVERY EPISODE, I WOULD WAIT TO SEE WHEN JOE WOULD SAY HIS LINE, "THE FACTS, JUST THE FACTS, MAM." JESUS HAD ALL THE FACTS ON THE SEVEN CHURCHES AND THE INDIVIDUALS THAT MADE THEM UP. AT THE END OF HIS FACT-FINDING SUMMARY, JESUS CRIES, "IF ANYONE HEARS MY INVITATION AND OPENS THE DOOR. I WILL COME IN TO HIM AND DINE WITH HIM AND HE WITH ME." JESUS IS KNOCKING ON THE DOOR OF YOUR HEART AND WANTS TO HAVE DINNER WITH YOU.

Nearly 90% of all resumes submitted for a job application possess some form of falsehood. These resumes contain a stretching of the facts or a downright lie! People will exaggerate their education, training, and years of experience. Jesus has the complete detailed accuracy of your spiritual condition and still wants to have fellowship with you. The invitation isn't reserved just for the pastors of the churches. Jesus says if anyone would hear my voice and if anyone would come to the door, we'll dine together.

In Matthew 11:28-30, Jesus gave a similar invitation when He said, "Come to Me, all you who labor and are heavy laden and I will give you rest. Take My yoke upon you and learn from Me, for I am gentle and lowly in heart, and you will find rest for your souls. For My yoke is easy and My burden is light." Aren't you glad Jesus didn't say, "Come to Me, all you who have your act together? Come to Me all who have a spotless resume? Come to Me all who don't need Me?" As Jesus stands at your door, know that life may be intense at times, but the hand that is knocking at your door is gentle. When you open the door, that gentle nail-scarred hand will be outstretched to you.

Listen for the knocking of the Savior one more time. Although the world presents us with clutter and noise pollution, open your ears to hear through the commotion. Jesus doesn't want to give you some new instructions to follow. He wants to transform your life. As you read the transformational truths each day, allow them to gently nudge you towards opening the door of fellowship and welcoming the Savior once again. "Anyone" is invited to the door.

REFLECT

Does your spiritual resume include spending time alone with Jesus every day in His Word, prayer, or song? If not, this is a place to begin.

Does your spiritual resume outline God's priorities for your life? Your priorities should include your intimate relationship with Jesus, then your family, and then your church.

Jesus already has the facts, and just the facts. Confession of sin begins by acknowledging that He has the facts. As you confess your sins to Jesus, He will help you rewrite your resume. What do you need to say to Him now?

DAY 15

A LESSON FROM EARL

*"If anyone hears my voice and opens the door,
I will come in to him…"*

Revelation 3:20

In this passage, Jesus is concluding one of seven letters that He has John send to His churches. John writes seven different copies of the book we call Revelation. He hand-writes a copy to Ephesus, Smyrna, Pergamos, Thyatira, Sardis, Philadelphia, and finally Laodicea. I can't help but think that John was praying over each church as He recorded and re-recorded the words of Jesus. Remember, John will be on the isle called Patmos for 18 months. He will have no contact with the churches to see how they respond. All we know is the plea that John makes at the end of each letter. "He who has an ear, let him hear what the Spirit is saying to the churches."

Note that John isn't saying that they can't hear, nor that they can't understand the message they have just heard. "Let him hear" recognizes the volition that you possess to choose to hear. The Bible, on several occasions, describes the fact that you can become hard of hearing. By repeatedly ignoring His voice, you become anesthetized to His voice. Up to this point, I've been focusing on the knocking. Jesus says that He not only knocks on the door, but He calls out to those inside to open the door. If you are His sheep, you know His voice.

TRANSFORMATIONAL TRUTH:
JESUS' VOICE REQUIRES ACTION ON YOUR PART!

YOU MUST NOT ONLY BE A HEARER OF THE WORD BUT A DOER OF THE WORD. JESUS SAYS IT'S NOT ENOUGH TO HEAR HIS VOICE (HEARER). YOU MUST OPEN THE DOOR (DOER). JESUS WANTS TO INVEST TIME IN YOU. IT'S A TRAGEDY IF YOU OFTEN ATTEMPT TO TALK TO JESUS BEHIND THE CLOSED DOOR.

I was blessed to have a wonderful Christian father-in-law. Earl was a humble, godly man who lived a simple life. I learned many lessons from Earl about life, in particular how people tend to make life too complicated. Instead of enjoying the simple, beautiful things that you often take for granted, you miss the moments in life where you get to spend time together. One thing that I most admired about Earl was that he always had time. Time to talk, to laugh, and to reminisce. I am ever in debt to him as he marveled about the changes in everything. He was born in 1909, and in his later years, Earl became very hard of hearing. Years of working in a brush factory left his hearing damaged and with each passing birthday, his hearing diminished even further. When Earl was 85, the family thought it would be a great idea to get him hearing aids. Earl hated the hearing aids. I can empathize with this as I needed to start wearing them myself when I turned 57. When Earl wore his hat or toboggan, he often forgot to turn the hearing aids off and would receive piercing feedback. He repaired bicycles for a hobby and part-time job, and always forgot to wash his hands before removing the hearing aids. For the most part, they brought a lot of unwanted noise into his very simple life. On one occasion, he was being encouraged (really nagged on) by his family to wear his hearing aids. We were all tired of yelling to communicate a message to him. After his wife and both daughters exhorted him and then left the room, Earl turned to me and spoke a profound statement. "Tom, I'm not hard of hearing, I'm tired of hearing!" I've never forgotten that moment.

There are times when I want to turn down the volume of those speaking to me. Their requests feel endless and I can never seem to meet their expectations. It is at those moments that I understand why Jesus would go up on the mountaintop to be alone. Please remember that the voice pleading you to open the door is a voice that you cannot afford to ignore, refuse, or reject. His voice alone can calm the storms and speak peace to your somewhat chaotic life. Seven letters to seven churches, all with the same plea! Please hear His voice, stop what you're doing, and open the door!

REFLECT

If you're guilty of ignoring His voice, then do as I did and repent! Will you ask Him to forgive your busyness? Have you ignored anyone around you and need to ask them for forgiveness too?

I have spent time in Baire, Cuba, training pastors and church leaders in the area of leadership, evangelism, and discipleship. I'm amazed at how simple life is there without all the distractions that I have in Ohio. A fresh truth that I've relearned and am reapplying is that when I'm too busy to hear His voice, busyness becomes a sin. Can I get a witness?

When you hear Jesus' voice, will you stop the business of your life and open the door for Him?

DAY 16

POT LUCK DINNERS

*"…I will come in to him and dine with him,
and he with Me."*

Revelation 3:20

As a pastor, when someone mentions dinner, I immediately think of pot-luck. Many in my denomination believe that if you can't make a green bean casserole, you're not allowed into Heaven! As a typical church kid growing up with multiple pot-luck dinners each month, my buddies and I would begin to notice the "better" dishes. Everyone would bring a specialty dish, but we quickly discovered that some weren't that special. We knew which casseroles were edible and which ones to avoid. We would always pick out our dessert first just in case the rapture came, and Jesus came to mess up my pot-luck. One of my favorite things to eat at pot-lucks was cornbread, and I would always find a couple of great extra crispy chicken legs. If there were soup beans, fried potato patties, or fresh greens beans available I was in hog heaven.

I reminisce about candlelight dinners with my wife at one of our favorite restaurants, or even better on a cruise ship suffering for Jesus in the Caribbean. In Cuba, dinner is at least a two-hour event where everything is prepared fresh from the moment you place your order. I have observed the same in Malawi, South Africa, Israel, and a multitude of other cultures around the world. "Come and dine" carries with it different connotations, to different people, in different cultures.

TRANSFORMATIONAL TRUTH:
JESUS WANTS TO SPEND TIME WITH YOU!

JESUS IS INTERESTED MORE IN THE CONVERSATION AROUND THE TABLE THAN THE MENU. HE MISSES HIS TIME WITH YOU AND INVITES YOU ONCE AGAIN TO ENJOY HIS PRESENCE AND COMPANY. THE ATMOSPHERE OF THE ROOM CHANGES WHEN JESUS IS PRESENT AS AN INVITED, WELCOMED, GUEST.

Jesus went to the home of His precious friends Mary, Martha, and Lazarus. Several guests had been invited as well since everyone desired an audience with Jesus. For some, they wanted favors and thought only of what Jesus could do for them, such as healing a particular disease. Others sought a blessing, came to criticize and observe Him from a distance, or hoped to see Him perform a miracle. Few in attendance came to sit with Him and be in His presence and company. Mary was the exception. Mary was found sitting at the feet of Jesus, listening and clinging to every word spoken. All that He said, she absorbed spiritually. Her sister Martha possessed the gift of hospitality. Everything had to be under her definition of perfect, providing the best place settings and comforts their home could afford. When Martha saw the behavior of Mary, she protested to Jesus. He gently spoke to Martha and gave her a valuable insight: cherish Me when I'm in your home. I want to spend time with you. The emphasis should always be on the time you spend together, not what the menu provides.

As Jesus stands at the door and knocks, calling your name over and over again, please know He's not hungry. He does not need you to whip up your specialty dish. He doesn't even want a cuppa, as my Australian friends would call it. Our Lord created manna, had it fall from the heavens, float above the ground, and kept up the process for forty years. There isn't anything you can make that will impress Him. Jesus desires you! Not something you can make, do, or provide. He only wants you! He misses the sound of your voice calling to Him in prayer. He misses the tears that fall upon the ground that He will keep. He misses your total dependence upon Him for the journey of each day that awaits you. Even though He rebuked and exhorted the Laodiceans, He still valued their time together!

REFLECT

Jesus desires to spend more time with you. What are three things that eat up your time and keep you from Him? Resolve to eliminate one of those three now!

Guess who's coming to dinner? As the head of your home, try to thank Him more for His presence than the food He provides!

Your time with Jesus is precious. Don't get caught up in the routines of life, but instead enjoy the God-moments He provides.

DAY 17

HE'S STILL WORKING ON ME

"Behold, I stand at the door and knock..."

Revelation 3:20

Jesus has several reasons in mind for standing at the door of your heart and continuously knocking. The top of the list is His never-ending love for you as He patiently waits for your reply. He persistently knocks at your door and He has promised to never leave you nor forsake you. Jesus knows the person that you are, but He also knows what you can become with Him at the center of your life. He will always remain faithful as He cannot change who He is no matter how unfaithful we may be to Him. God keeps His word!

Jesus wants you to unlock the door; He still sees the potential that lies within you. He has your resume and still believes in you. As a child growing up, I adored gospel music, especially Southern Gospel music. I loved to hear the quartets with a tenor who sang up in the rafters with his high voice, and the bass that would vibrate the speakers as he belched out low notes. Family harmony was by far my favorite style, as no one can harmonize better than a family. The family of my mother-in-law, Vivian, come from the foothills of Kentucky. Vivian had twelve siblings who could all sing quite well. Down home, we used to call it front porch singing when families would sit around and sing the songs of Zion. The harmony was incredible as the Holy Spirit descended and we worshiped sitting there on the porch. One of my favorite family groups, The Hemphills, sang down home music. One of the members, Joel, wrote several of their songs. My favorite song that he wrote is entitled, "He's Still Working on Me." As you read these lyrics, let them sink in for just a moment to the fact that God sees the potential that lies within you. He hasn't given up on you.

"He's still working on me
To make me what I ought to be
It took Him just a week to make the moon and the stars
The sun and the earth and Jupiter and Mars
How loving and patient He must be
Cause He's still working on me

There really ought to be a sign upon my heart
Don't judge me yet there's an unfinished part
But I'll be perfect just according to His plan
Fashioned by the Master's loving hands

He's still working on me
To make me what I ought to be
It took Him just a week to make the moon and the stars
The sun and the earth and Jupiter and Mars
How loving and patient He must be
Cause He's still working on me

In the mirror of His word
Reflections that I see
Makes me wonder why He never gave up on me
But He loves me as I am and helps me when I pray
Remember He's the potter I'm the clay

He's still working on me
To make me what I ought to be
It took Him just a week to make the moon and the stars
The sun and the earth and Jupiter and Mars
How loving and patient He must be
Cause He's still working on me"

TRANSFORMATIONAL TRUTH:
ALLOW YOUR SELF-ESTEEM TO BE WHAT JESUS
THINKS OF YOU.

HE HASN'T GIVEN UP ON YOU AND HE NEVER WILL. HE KNOWS YOU BY NAME. HE KNOWS YOUR FAILURES AND SUCCESSES. HE KNOWS YOUR FEAR AND PAIN. HE SEES THE VALUE THAT YOU ARE TO HIM AND HIS KINGDOM. OPEN THE DOOR TODAY. THE ANGELS WILL BE APPLAUDING, AND THE CLOUD OF WITNESSES ARE CHEERING YOU ON.

Paul told Timothy to "stir up" the gift that lay within him when Timothy became weary in his well doing. He was tired of the criticism and was considering quitting. Paul saw the potential that lay in his young son of the faith. He encouraged Timothy to persevere. Paul looked through earthly eyes and saw the potential in Timothy. Jesus looks through divine eyes and knows your potential! He will never give up on you or stop knocking on the door of your heart.

REFLECT

What is one small step that you can make today towards opening the door of your heart and allowing Christ in?

The Potter isn't finished with your life. He wants to mold it into something that brings Him glory. What gifting, that lies within you, needs to be "stirred up?"

If your self-esteem has been broken by others, will you turn to Jesus today and allow Him to heal your pain? You are a new creation in Christ, and He values spending time with you.

IV

THE DOORS OF
SEXUAL IMMORALITY

Proverbs 5

Scripture warns us to avoid the door of sexual immorality. It is a guarantee of disaster, divorce, and disappointment. It is a door of deception, designed to ensnare and entrap those who shun its warning. This is a no-nonsense door. One that cannot be compromised with at any stage, or age, in life. It is a door that has no sense of respect. It kills, steals, and destroys all who enter.

Take these days of devotion to become intimate with Jesus Christ and listen to the guiding of the Holy Spirit. Allow the confrontation that this door brings, to purge your thought life, and purify your mind. Sanctify yourself and determine never to go near this attractive, flirtatious door. This is not the door of a friend, but a door of fantasy. All who enter inside become victims and casualties!

DAY 18

KEEP YOUR EYES ON HIM

*"Remove your way far from her, and do not
go near the door of her house"*

Proverbs 5:8

Have you ever been warned about something only to blow it off later? The warning was stern, intense, and clearly communicated. You thought it wouldn't affect you, or change your life in any way. Once you decided to ignore their advice, you got in over your head. You soon realized that you had been deceived. Deception is one of the primary tactics of any adversary. Satan's strategy has always been deception. In the garden of Eden, he approached Eve and questioned what God had said to her.

When I played little league baseball, I was the lead-off hitter. My job was to get on base by any means including a hit, walk, or get beaned (which is being hit with the ball by the pitcher). In one of our more

75

important games, I completed a clutch single. We were trailing by one run, and my job was simple. I had to either steal second base for an ideal scoring position, or advance to third if a ball was hit to the outfield. My primary responsibility was to keep my eye on the third base coach. He directed everything on the field. The next batter hit a line drive into the right-center field. As the ball cleared the second basemen, I took off, failing to keep my eye on the coach. As I approached the second base, the shortstop began to cover the bag as if he was waiting on the throw from the outfielder. I followed my instincts and training by sliding head-first into second base to beat the tag. To my sudden surprise, he moved out of my way. I realized I had been deceived. Stark reality soon set in as I looked to my third-base coach who was in religious terms, "grieved in his spirit." Actually, he wasn't grieved, he was slightly upset and frantically motioning me to third base. I got to my feet, made it to third base, to face the wrath of my coach. He helped brush the dirt off me, turned me around towards home, and then proceeded to kick me in the rear-end!

You say: Pastor, I thought we were talking about sexual immorality? Let me finish the story. Fortunately, the next batter hit a ball over the left field wall, and we won the game. That event taught me a valuable lesson. Always keep my eye on the coach. It's a part of my life, but the deception I experienced in the little league didn't scar me for life. Some decisions teach valuable lessons; others can scar you for the rest of your life. Our team would have been disappointed had we lost the game, but the door of sexual immorality not only destroys your integrity, reputation, and character, but the lives of the innocent in your sphere of influence. Your family, church, neighbors, co-workers will be affected by sinful choices and selfish desires. This is the warning regarding this door. The Proverb said do not even go near the house!

**TRANSFORMATIONAL TRUTH:
LISTEN WHEN GOD SAYS GO AND
WHEN HE SAYS NO.**

WHEN GOD'S WORD SAYS "THOU SHALT," YOU HAVE A GREEN LIGHT FROM GOD. WHEN GOD'S WORD SAYS "THOU SHALT NOT," IT'S A CLEAR, RED SIGNAL TO STOP. HE DOES NOT USE ANY CAUTION LIGHTS. IF YOU OPEN THE DOOR, IT CONTAINS PAIN, DECEIT, SICKNESS, DISEASE, AND BROKENNESS. BY WARNING, GOD IS TRYING TO PROTECT NOT ONLY YOU, BUT OTHERS FROM THE PAIN, EMBARRASSMENT, AND DIS-APPOINTMENT THIS DOOR CAUSES.

As you explore the warning attached to this door, please know that God's grace can forgive and restore your broken fellowship with the Holy Spirit. The scripture says in 1 John 1:9, "if we confess our sins, He is faithful and just to forgive us our sins, and to cleanse us from *all* unrighteousness." Fellowship and trust by those closest to you is a different matter. It may take time to see restoration occur.

REFLECT

If you're tempted to open this door, the scripture gives one unmistakable piece of advice: RUN! Do not open the door or it will cost you more than you're willing to pay.

If you're in over your head, there is still time to come home! What red light is God giving you?

Trust the Holy Spirit to guide you to the truth. His convicting persistence is a demonstration of His love. He hates the sin, but not the sinner. Keep your eye on the coach!

DAY 19

ONLY BY GRACE

"Keep your distance from such a woman;
absolutely stay out of her neighborhood."

Proverbs 5:8 (MSG)

What does the word "far" mean to you? To me, it is simply the opposite of near. It doesn't take a theological debate or biblical commentary to understand that far is the opposite of near! If you are near, what will it take for you to distance yourself? God clearly tells you to stay far away from the door of sexual immorality. As my mother used to say when she was trying to emphasize a point or restrain her frustration, "It's as plain as the nose on my face!"

Why do you have a tendency to doubt the consequences of your actions? In the garden of Eden, Satan told Eve that if she ate the forbidden fruit, she would not die. That is when the game of deception began, and continues today. A frequent statement regarding children who are casualties of adulterous affairs is that "the kids will be fine." After thirty years of listening to broken lives, I can emphatically say that the children are not fine. They are broken, confused, and ashamed. They blame themselves, sometimes for years, for their parent's break-up. The pain is very real, and nothing can mask their suffering. Only the Holy Spirit can heal that hurt and speak peace to their lives again. You never forget it; you can only make peace with the situation.

In Proverbs seven, the Bible states that "He did not know it would *cost* his life." I've heard many say that "No matter what the cost, it was worth it." In other words, many feel entitled to have their lust and desires fulfilled. After the initial deception wears off, you realize the pain that your selfish desire causes. The ripple effect of your decision reaches farther than you could imagine, and the consequences of deception begin. This byproduct has a term that needs no commentary or theological explanation. The fruit of deception is guilt. Guilt: that nagging reality that you have committed a shameful act. The case has been tried, and the verdict rendered.

TRANSFORMATIONAL TRUTH:
GUILT CAN ONLY BE FORGIVEN BY GRACE!

THERE IS NO WAY TO EARN OR DESERVE GRACE. THE SAME WAY YOU GOT INTO THE PLAN OF GOD, IS THE SAME THING THAT SUSTAINS YOU IN HIS PLAN. GRACE IS A BLESSING OF UNDESERVED FAVOR. GOD'S GRACE IS TRULY AMAZING WHEN IT SAVES AND IS OVERWHELMING AS IT SUSTAINS. NO MATTER WHAT YOU'VE DONE, HIS GRACE WILL FORGIVE.

In 1986, my wife and I separated. There wasn't adultery, another woman, or another man involved, but I was running from God. I was miserable to be around. I waited until my two little girls went to bed, took two green garbage bags to pack my clothes, and made the drive to my parent's home. I had been advised by others to get mad, get an attorney, and fight for everything I could keep. Make sure the advice you're receiving from your friends, co-workers, and even relatives are biblical. The only person walking with the Lord was my mother. She continually prayed, fasted, and interceded for her son, daughter-in-law, and her two granddaughters.

During our six-month separation, I heard the nagging voice of my pride, and the temptation to move on became very real. In the garden, Satan appealed to the pride of both Adam and Eve by telling them they would become "like" God. I felt like a failure and a miserable father. I had regret and guilt for not being the spiritual leader of my home. I'm grateful that I listened to the council of the Lord, through my mother. If I got right with God and trusted Him for my future, He could heal my home. It is a blessing that God protected me from any door where I did not belong. Keep your distance from temptation and resist the door that God asks you to keep closed.

REFLECT

If you don't have accountability in regards to the purity of your marriage, ask God to send you a trusted friend or family member to give you wise counsel. Give them permission to ask any tough questions.

Is there a safe distance between you and temptation? If you're going in opposite directions you never have to fear passing each other in the dark.

The byproduct of grace is restoration. Relationships are restored through grace.

DAY 20
WHEN IGNORANCE ISN'T BLISS

"...you do not know them...he did not know it would cost his life."

Proverbs 5:6, 23

When Donna and I were separated, people were telling me to fight so I wouldn't lose anything. They did not realize that I had already lost everything important to me: Donna, Jessica, and Vanessa. Material possessions didn't matter anymore. My relationship with my wife broke; my children didn't understand why daddy was living with mama and papa! Vacations memories were going in different directions. Thanksgiving and Christmas took on new meanings. All this took place, and sexual immorality wasn't even involved! Everything I had ever called normal was now damaged.

"Ignorance is bliss" is a phrase coined in the 18th century and essentially says this: What you don't know cannot hurt you. When it comes to sexual immorality, the phrase doesn't apply. Once you open that door and step through the threshold, it slams shut behind you, and your life is forever changed. When Paul wrote to Corinth, he challenged the church to be aware of their adversities. "Lest Satan should *take* advantage of us; for we are not ignorant of his devices." (2 Cor. 2:11) Ignorance of sexual immoralities can cause tremendous hardships in your life through the exchange of your life's plan, integrity, and possessions.

The term, *lest,* describes the possibility of an undesirable consequence. In ignorance, you face a scenario similar to that in Proverbs 5:6. "Lest you ponder her path of life—Her ways are unstable; You do not *know* them." Opening this door will poison your life. There is an exchange process that takes place when this sin originates. You exchange your current direction in life and take a detour that leads to a dead-end!

The second situation challenges your integrity. Integrity has been defined in many ways, but typically is represented as who you are when no one is looking. Whether it's physical, emotional, or digital, sexual immorality steals a man's honor. "Lest you give your honor to others, and your years to the cruel one." (Prov. 5:9) The exchange through this threshold takes your reputation, respect, and self-esteem and gives them into the hands of others. Your name will never be the same. The prime of your life is taken from you, as you focus on being blackmailed and held hostage to guilt. Ignorance produces relationships that will never be the same!

The final exchange takes your possessions. What was once yours, is now someone else's. My children could be calling someone else daddy! "Lest aliens be filled with your wealth, and your labors go to the house of a foreigner." (Prov. 5:10) What used to be yours, is now theirs. Alimony, child-support, portfolio's, houses, stocks, and bonds; nothing is left untouched as the door slams shut behind you!

**TRANSFORMATIONAL TRUTH:
REPENTANCE IS THE *ONLY* ANTIDOTE FOR
SEXUAL IMMORALITY.**

WHEN YOU REPENT, CONFESS YOUR SIN WITHOUT EXCUSES OR MODIFICATION OF TERMS. REPENT TO GOD WITH THE TRUTH. THIS RESULTS IN GODLY SORROW THAT CULMINATES INTO A CHANGE OF BEHAVIOR. EVERYTHING MUST BE CONFESSED: GENUINE REPENTANCE DOESN'T CARE WHO KNOWS! WHEN GENUINE REPENTANCE TAKES PLACE, YOU'RE GLAD TO BE RIGHT WITH GOD. A RIGHT RELATIONSHIP WITH GOD CAN LEAD TO A RIGHT RELATIONSHIP WITH OTHERS.

You need to uncover ignorance and face reality living. Not all relationships can be mended, and not everyone will be fine. This door causes pain, stress, depression, addictions, and loss. Grace and repentance are the only cure and your only hope.

REFLECT

If you have an issue with overeating, don't stand in front of the Twinkie section at the grocery store. You'll lose every time. The Bible says, do not go near the sexually immoral door of "her" house. Stay as far away as you can, or you may fail.

How do you rebuild a broken life? The same way Nehemiah rebuilt the walls of Jerusalem. Pour a new foundation and lay one brick at a time. It's hard work, but it's worth it!

Take an honest assessment of yourself. If you are ensnared in the world of video, digital, or technological sexual immorality, seek help now!

DAY 21

A MATTER OF THE HEART

*"Remove your way from her, and do not
go near the door of her house."*

Proverbs 5:8

As you meditate on this door today, make sure you understand that both men and women struggle with sexual immorality. Both genders are addicted to pornography. While scripture addresses the man, its consequences find common ground with ladies. Solomon writes as he walks down the streets of Jerusalem, observing life. His father, David, had been known as "a man after God's own heart," yet David fell victim to this door. His son Solomon would fall prey also.

*"If Solomon had stored these proverbs in his heart
instead of in his head, he would have gone down in
history as the greatest of all kings."*

John Phillips, Exploring Proverbs

Quit avoid the question, dancing around the answer, or changing the subject! Pastor, what's the question? Here it is; "Where's your heart?" Sexual immorality is a spiritual issue. No matter what started you down the wrong neighborhood, the heart is always involved. Maybe you've taken your spouse for granted. This could be an area of weakness, just as others struggle with alcohol, drugs, gambling, gossip, etc. Communication breaks down in marriage as you stray from the basics of prayer, scripture reading, small groups, serving others, and sacrificial giving. An entitlement mindset creeps in, and before you know it, you're standing in front of the wrong house getting ready to walk inside. Many times, the thought has run through your mind that "this will never happen to me," only to succumb to temptation at a later time.

**TRANSFORMATIONAL TRUTH:
SATAN CREATES TEMPTATION SPECIFICALLY
FOR YOU.**

THE INVITATION TO BECOME A "FRIEND" WITH SOMEONE ON FACEBOOK IN TODAY'S WORLD CAN BE SATAN'S MOST POPULAR CHOICE OF SEDUCTION. YOU DO NOT UNDERSTAND THE HIDDEN AGENDA: SHE DOESN'T WANT TO BE YOUR FRIEND, SHE WANTS TO BE YOUR FANTASY! WHEN THE GRASS LOOKS GREENER AT THE OTHER HOUSE, REMEMBER THAT THERE IS A SEPTIC TANK THAT LIES JUST UNDER THE SURFACE.

There is a high cost to low living: bitter, wormwood (poison), death, Hell, unstable, cruel, mourn, flesh consumed, body consumed, despised, seduced, deceived, entrapped, astray, ignorance, wounded, slaughter, and destruction. All of these are on the menu of sexual immorality. These traits are not posted on the door as a sign of warning to you. You must be cautious and recognize what the door of sexual immorality holds within.

> "For she has cast down many wounded, and all who were slain by her were strong men."
>
> Proverbs 7:26

The book of Proverbs addresses three different types of people: The wise, the fools, and the scoffers. The wise are identified as those who know God and who follow his commands. The fools do not know God and do not keep His commandments. The scoffers reject God and make fun of His people of faith. When it comes to sexual immorality, no one has the last laugh. The wise are heartbroken from the pain this door causes. The fools could care less about the consequences since they have hope in this life only. The scoffers point out the failures of others, even mocking them. They look down on those who walk with the Lord in belittlement and pity. When followers of Christ walk through the door and become casualties, the scoffers will gloat, deride, and make fun of their pain. Where's your heart? Turn your heart towards home today. Listen to the warning of scripture and do not flirt with the door of sexual immorality.

REFLECT

Do you have a daily plan to read through scripture each year? You can find many online. Begin reading scripture and allow scripture to lead you.

When temptation comes your way, there are ways to move forward wisely. Call your spouse to hear their voice. Change the scenery to focus on your kids or grandkids. Keep their pictures close, as a precious gift from the Lord.

Do whatever it takes to keep yourself from sexual immorality. Change careers, friends, or neighborhoods if necessary. There is nothing worth losing your family or your integrity.

V

THE DOOR TO HEAVEN

Revelation 4:1-3

Revelation describes the door to Heaven through the eyes of John, the beloved disciple of Jesus. This door reminds you of one incredible truth: One day your faith will become sight! Whether you have to walk through the valley of the shadow of death, or are alive and remain when Jesus calls His bride home, this door provides one clear message: Jesus Wins!

As your eternal High Priest, Jesus is interceding for you and is preparing a place for you to dwell for eternity. Revelation four presents the reality that you have known all along. God keeps His word! He uses a trumpet, a door, a throne, jewelry, and a rainbow to strengthen your resolve until He comes. Patmos was John's temporary address; the third Heaven will be his permanent home!

DAY 22

AFTER THESE THINGS

"After these things I looked and behold, a door standing open in heaven. And the first voice I heard was like a trumpet talking with me, saying, 'Come up Here, and I will show you things which must take place after this.'"

Revelation 4:1-3

Other than His parents, we can imply from scripture that there was no one closer to Jesus than His beloved disciple, John. He had seen Jesus open the eyes of the blind and unlock the ears of the deaf. He witnessed Jesus cleanse the leapers, calm the seas, and feed 20,000 people with a little boy's sack lunch. John had never observed Jesus as the conquering King who is coming to reign on Earth. "After these things" transitions into a time where John has seen Jesus in his vision of the second coming. He sees his friend and Savior coming to rightfully reclaim Earth from the prince of the powers of this age, Satan himself. John hasn't seen Jesus in over sixty years. The reality of this event startled John to the point where he pretended to faint. Jesus picks up His beloved disciple, dusts him off, and speaks. He tells John not to fear for He has conquered death, hell, and the grave.

John was understandably in shock over what he had just witnessed with his own eyes. Jesus commissions John to write the things he saw. He wrote have seven letters, sent to seven different churches, in the land which is now modern-day Turkey. These letters give a DNA overview of the church throughout the centuries. John is then transported off the isle of Patmos and into the third Heaven to record what must take place hereafter. He begins with a simple, yet very complex phrase, "after these things."

"After these things" indicates previous, significant events that you leave behind, and move towards moments yet to be experienced. It refers to a time after cancer, heart attacks, automobile accidents, and divorces. After graduating from high school or college, her saying yes to your proposal, or the birth of your first child. Nothing is ever the same after you have lived through these events. "After these things" statements can summarize your life before you found Christ. You are not the same person you were; you became a new creation in Christ Jesus.

TRANSFORMATIONAL TRUTH:
THE BIBLE IS HISTORY WRITTEN IN ADVANCE.

YOUR FUTURE IS ALREADY TAKING PLACE. THE REALITY OF REVELATION IS THAT GOD HAS A PLAN. HIS PLAN CANNOT BE STOPPED. ONE DAY, HIS PLAN WILL

PLACE YOU IN HIS FATHER'S HOUSE TO BE IN THE PRESENCE OF JESUS FOR ALL OF ETERNITY. "AFTER THESE THINGS" WILL SHUT ONE DOOR SO YOU CAN BE LEAD TO YOUR FUTURE, AND OPEN ANOTHER DOOR OF TRANSFORMATION. THIS DOOR TAKES YOUR BODY OF CORRUPTION AND EXCHANGES IT TO BE INCORRUPTIBLE. YOUR MORTAL BODY CHANGES TO A FORM THAT IS IMMORTAL. YOUR FUTURE IS NOT ONLY SECURE, BUT IT IS GOING TO BLOW YOUR MIND. THE EYE HAS NOT SEEN, EAR HAS NOT HEARD, NEITHER HAS IT ENTERED INTO THE HEART OF MAN THE THINGS THAT GOD HAS PREPARED FOR HIM. I CAN ONLY IMAGINE.

John's "after these things" statement is accumulative of all that has gone on in the church since the day of Pentecost until the rapture of the church. The rapture will be the next great prophetic event to take place in the life of the church. The bride of Christ will be summoned home as a bride adorned for her Husband. Right now, you are still living during a part of the "after these things" journey.

REFELCT

Has Jesus ever stooped down and lifted you up by His right hand of favor? How can you help others by sharing that blessing today?

If the church were to run her course today, and the rapture of the church took place, would you be left behind or would you walk through the open door in Heaven?

The invitation to come up here is for those who recognize His voice, and your faith becomes sight. For the child of God, your future is in front of you and it is not about what's behind.

DAY 23
HOMESICK FOR HEAVEN

*"…'Come up here, and I will show you things
which must take place after this.'"*

Revelation 4:1

I'm a homebody and proud to admit it. As Dorothy once said, "There's no place like home, there's no place like home!" I have been privileged to travel all over the world and see more things than the average person. Numerous continents, countries, and Caribbean islands have been a part of my itinerary, but one overarching theme remains. It's not home. My most recent per se crisis was in Baire, Cuba while speaking to pastors from the Eastern Convention of Cuba. We flew to Miami on Monday and arrived in Cuba on Tuesday to begin our ministry. By the time Sunday evening had passed, I had taught for two full days, preached six times, and had met numerous pastors that Urbancrest is privileged to support. As Sunday evening was winding down, we realized that Monday was going to be, for the most part, an off day. My colleague and I began to discuss our homesick issues. I loved pouring into the pastors, missionaries, and leaders. I was witnessing God move in incredible ways as eleven people gave their lives to Jesus on Sunday. I knew Monday wouldn't be the same, as my heart was already heading home to my wife and granddaughter. I hate to admit it, but I even missed our three dogs Theo, Dolly, and Charlie who are affectionately referred to by me as dumb, dumber, and dumbest.

**TRANSFORMATIONAL TRUTH:
MY HEART ACHES FOR HOME!**

AS MUCH AS OHIO HAS BEEN MY HOME FOR 62 YEARS, I'M STILL NOT HOME. THERE IS GROANING AND KNOWING WITHIN THAT TELLS ME I DON'T BELONG HERE. AS A CHILD OF GOD, YOU WILL NEVER BE SATISFIED WITH THE THINGS OF THIS EARTH AS ALL OF HEAVEN AWAITS.

As a little boy, I began to hear about the return of Jesus Christ at what our pastor called the Rapture of the church. "In a moment, in the twinkling of an eye" Jesus will call His church home. I grew up reading God's Word daily. I would hear my mother sing about Heaven and all that was awaiting us there. Church taught me that one day we would receive an entirely new body. This teaching seemed to excite the adults, but especially the senior adults. At the time, I didn't understand what all the big deal was about, but I certainly can relate now! Revelation 4 ushers us into the throne room of God for a preview of coming attractions. Before John attempts to describe a throne, pieces of jewelry, and a rainbow, He gathers our attention with the cry "behold." John saw a door opened in Heaven and a trumpet-like voice shouting for us to come home. For over two thousand years the church has been awaiting that cry.

I have often tried to place myself in the shoes of those who penned the scriptures. John says that he was transported into the third Heaven immediately. He is recording these events with the realization that He has to go back to the Isle of Patmos. Tomorrow he will wake up and begin digging once again in a salt mine exiled from the world. The beloved disciple will not be set free for some time. Thoughts must have flooded his mind knowing that he didn't belong there. The history of all mankind was sketched forever in his mind. He knew that he no longer belonged on Patmos, Ephesus, or any other city on Earth. He belonged in the city of God! John spoke five words that summarized a vision of ecstasy, splendor, triumph, and terror. "Even so, come Lord Jesus!" My heart aches for home also. After this time on Earth, you're going home to where you finally have a sense of belonging.

REFLECT

Can you recall the time when you were "homesick" the most? I pray that same feeling is born in you as you wait for His voice.

If Jesus called you home today, would those closest to you go home also? Will you share with them the good news of the gospel of Jesus Christ?

Does John's statement "Even so, come Lord Jesus" concern you or excite you? I'm concerned for those who don't know Him but I'm excited for those who do!

DAY 24

ONE SAT ON THE THRONE

"…behold, a throne set in heaven,
and One sat on the throne."

Revelation 4:2

Many have claimed to be God. Many have seen themselves as the greatest. The list is seemingly endless of those who thought they were the greatest. In the arena of sports one heavy-weight fighter made a poem of his so-called greatness:

"Float like a butterfly
Sting like a bee
I am the greatest
I'm Mohammed Ali!"

Even fairy tale stories have gotten involved with the question of greatness:

THROUGH THE DOOR

"Mirror, Mirror on the wall
Who's the fairest of them all?"

All of John's attention is immediately drawn to a single, occupied throne in Heaven. Heavenly thrones signify supreme authority and rulership for all eternity. A single throne implies absolute rulership. A throne speaks of a kingdom. The One seated on the throne is to be revered by His servants.

TRANSFORMATIONAL TRUTH:
JESUS HAS NO RIVALS.

HE ALONE IS SEATED ON THE THRONE. HE ALONE IS JUDGE. ALL KINGS AND QUEENS OF THIS EARTH WILL BOW BEFORE HIM. SATAN AND ALL THE DEMONIC HOSTS OF HELL WILL COWER AND CRY JESUS IS LORD. HE SHALL REIGN FOREVER AND EVER, AMEN! THE NEXT TIME SATAN REMINDS YOU OF YOUR PAST, REMIND HIM OF HIS FUTURE. WE ARE JOINT-HEIRS WITH CHRIST TO THE THRONE IN HEAVEN!

The throne room of God is a dominant theme in the book of Revelation. What makes your relationship with Jesus precious is that His throne is accessible to all who believe. Jesus promises the overcomer to sit with Him, on His throne, even as He is seated at the right hand of the Father. Access to Jesus' throne is of great spiritual emphasis and causes tremendous spiritual warfare on Earth. You were created lower than the angels, yet have access to God's throne. Simply put, Satan is jealous of human beings.

Before the fall of Satan, one of his primary responsibilities was to stand watch over the throne of God. In his heart, his pride caused him to proclaim he would exalt his throne above the stars of God. One of the great misconceptions regarding this fallen creature is that he now rules in Hell and sits on a throne giving commands to the demons of Hell. Allow this thought to sink in: Satan has never been to Hell, nor does he have a throne from which he rules. Satan will spend all of eternity in the lake of fire with all the fallen angels, alongside all of fallen, unsaved mankind. He isn't robed in a little red suit, carrying a red pitchfork, and breathing fire. He avoids the place which holds a constant reminder of his future, Hell. One day, all of his temporal authority will be stripped away. He will be seen as a fallen created being who rebelled against God. The inhabitants of Hell will ask this question, "Is this the one who made the Earth tremble, who shook kingdoms?" Satan has failed in all his promises to reign. All of Hell mourns because there is no authority to turn to for deliverance. Jesus' Name will be exalted to that of highest honor and respect. Today, Satan is still the temporal ruler of this Earth, but his reign has a limited term.

Satan attacks the believer with relentless fury because you, as an inferior creation, will one day be clothed with a body of resurrection like Jesus' body. You will have unfettered access to the throne of God. Satan will have an eternity of regrets; you will have an eternity of rewards. Jesus has no rivals! His throne is righteous and holy. You will serve Him for all of eternity.

REFLECT

Who is number one in your life? Jesus Christ is Lord, you are His servant.

Jesus has no rivals. When you allow other people, things, or circumstances to come between your relationship with Him Jesus calls them idols. How does Revelation 4:1-2 allow the Holy Spirit to give you a fresh view of your exalted Savior?

Satan will always attempt to get you to focus on your past because he has already seen where you will spend your future. When Satan attacks, remind him of your allegiance to Jesus!

DAY 25

METAPHORS OF ETERNITY

"And He who sat there was like a jasper and a sardius stone in appearance; and there was a rainbow around the throne, in appearance like and emerald."

Revelation 4:3

John is transported into the third Heaven and sees a singular, majestic throne where the One is seated. As John fixes his eyes on the throne, he begins to use metaphors to describe what he saw. These metaphors were very familiar and recognizable to the audience who would read his letter.

John begins to describe the precious stones of jasper and sardius which were of tremendous significance to the nation of Israel. The High Priest of Israel wore a breastplate of twelve stones, each representing one of the twelve tribes. The first and last stones are symbols of God's sovereignty over His chosen people of Israel. As John was ushered through the door of Heaven, his eyes fell upon the eternal high priest, Jesus. The scriptures declare that He lives to make intercession for you. As the eternal high priest, Jesus offered up the sacrifice of Himself, once and for all. When He ascended into Heaven, Jesus was given the position of highest honor and sat on the throne of God.

> *"Therefore He is also able to save to the uttermost those who come to God through Him, since He always lives to make intercession for them."*
>
> *Hebrews 7:25*

Without a moment's pause, John takes the description of Jesus to another level as he witnesses a rainbow that encircles the throne. The rainbow has been a pillar to the people of God, since its creation by God. The rainbow exists as a sign that has one singular message; God keeps His word. God made a covenant promise to Noah that He would never again destroy the Earth by a flood. It was a sign that He would never go back on His word. The rainbow points to one of the attributes of God Himself, His veracity. Veracity boldly proclaims that God is absolute truth. He always keeps His word!

Imagine what John is trying to describe as he is overwhelmed by one dominant color of the rainbow that encircles God's throne. The emerald, a translucent green gemstone. Colors have great biblical significance in scripture and green speaks of life, and in this case, eternal life.

TRANSFORMATIONAL TRUTH:
YOU CAN TAKE GOD AT HIS WORD!

THE DOOR OPENED IN HEAVEN IS GOD'S GUARAN-TEE OF ETERNAL SALVATION. JOHN SAW JESUS ALONE, SEATED ON THE THRONE AS THE ETERNAL HIGH PRIEST, THE SAVIOR WHO KEEPS HIS WORD AND PROVIDES THE ONLY PATH OF ETERNAL LIFE.

One day the promises of Heaven will be yours. On this Earth, you are instructed in scripture to walk by faith, not by sight. John gives reassurance that your faith will one day become sight. You will walk through the door of Heaven and dwell there for all of eternity. John's description of Jesus is also a solemn warning to all who would trust in anyone or anything other than Jesus Christ. He shed His blood as a payment for your sins and entrance into Heaven. Jesus alone is sovereign. Jesus alone offers the only way off of Earth and into Heaven. Jesus alone is absolute truth. Jesus alone is encircled by an emerald rainbow of life.

John recorded the events in Heaven as an encouragement and warning. Behold the majesty of the One who is seated on the throne and allow Heaven's open door to transform your life. John gave a sneak preview of coming attractions where He's preparing a place that you can only imagine.

REFLECT

If someone asked you to describe Jesus using earthly metaphors what kind of picture would you paint?

If you're wondering today if God is listening or if you can take God at His word, the next time you observe the beauty of a rainbow let it remind you of His veracity and faithfulness.

Jesus is making intercession for you. No matter your circumstances, will you trust that He will not give up on you? John says that Jesus talks to the Father about your needs. Let me encourage you to talk with Him today!

VI

THE DOORS OF ADVERSITY

1 Corinthians 16:8-13

In the realities of everyday life; you get sick, have surgeries, feel misunderstood, maligned, and mistreated. When this door opens, you face a door that holds both the positive and negative inside. Some are doors that will open for you to grow as a disciple of Christ. That open door brings opposition from Satan. Spiritual warfare becomes a reality with both successes and failures along the way.

Adversity comes from within and without. At times, I'm my own worst enemy by the daily choices I make and by underestimating my opponent. This is hand-to-hand combat. Paul uses wrestling as a metaphor to describe the battle of the mind, the will, and the soul. You must take an honest assessment of your past to open up doors of promise for the future.

DAY 26

YOU ARE HERE

"But I will tarry in Ephesus until Pentecost.
For a great and effective door has opened to me,
and there are many adversaries."

1 Corinthians 16:8-9

I am directionally impaired. I have no built-in system or internal GPS. Since I'm also technologically impaired, I must depend upon my navigator and copilot. Also known as my wife, Donna. If Donna isn't with me it's a miracle that I can get from one location to another. We live very close to an incredible amusement park called Kings Island. It is a child's paradise and provides rides for almost every age conceivable. Better yet, it has a world class water park with wave pools, a lazy river, and more slides than you can imagine. There are times when we take the entire family, along with the grandchildren and our great-grandson. Inevitably, I will get turned around. I should just be a realist and proudly yell out "LOST!" One thing that I learned early on is that I'm not the only dork in the park that gets lost. At certain intersections, they have a large map with a big red dot that says, "YOU ARE HERE!" If I know where I am and where I need to go I can get back on course. Before you can ever get back to the course you need to be on, take a moment to be a realist. You need to recognize where you are.

I love all of scripture, but I especially admire the writings of Paul. He displayed the good, the bad, and the ugly. Paul was a realist. At times he was very transparent, even raw in his delivery, yet always real. Paul didn't have any false humility and never attempted to face the adversaries alone. He begged people to pray for him, and that others would spread the gospel to the ends of the Earth.

What is an adversary? In the basic definition, an adversary is a person who opposes or fights against another; opponent; enemy. Adversary suggests an enemy who fights determinedly, continuously, and relentlessly. Paul, when writing to Corinth a second time, stated: "lest Satan should take advantage of us; for we are not ignorant of his devices." (2 Cor. 2:11)

Anytime you take the step of faith, to walk through the door of spiritual growth, you must be acutely aware that this same door will come with a price. The price tag is an adversary who is determined to keep you from moving forward in intimacy with Christ. An adversary who uses any method available to see your growth halted before it can produce fruit. There is no low to which he will not stoop, and no method of attack that he will leave in his arsenal unused. His plan is to steal, kill, and destroy. This has been an effective strategy since the Garden of Eden. He moves forward with great resolve to destroy lives, homes, marriages, families, and children. He has no moral boundary that is off limits. No conscience that would tell him that you've had enough for one day and he needs to lighten. His job is to fascinate and then assassinate; to thrill and then to kill.

Paul was neither an optimist or a pessimist; he was a realist. He was facing organized, systematic idolatry. It all centered around the famous temple of Diana in the name of religion. They would promote ritual prostitution and sexual perversion as euphoric, religious experiences. Paul faced a culture of wine, women, and song. Paganism, occultism, demonism, superstition, sex trafficking, racism, and brutal forms of slavery. He was verbally, physically, and spiritually abused from the moment he set foot in the city. Paul chose to stay three years in that atmosphere before turning the church over to young Timothy, who the church and city chewed up and spit out. Apollos (1 Corinthians 16:12) was next in line to replace Timothy. Apollos refused to return, even though Paul begged with him. He may have even used a now popular song to express his true feelings: "Na-Na-Na-Na-Na-Na-Na-Na-Hey-Hey-goodbye!"

**TRANSFORMATIONAL TRUTH:
YOUR OWN THOUGHTS CAN BE AN ENEMY.**

THE AVERAGE CHRISTIAN IS SO MENTALITY UNSTABLE THAT ADVERSARY CAN LEAVE YOU ALONE. THERE IS NO NEED FOR VERBAL OR EVEN PHYSICAL ABUSE AS LONG AS YOU LET THE ENEMY CONTROL YOUR THOUGHTS. THIS KEEPS YOU IN BONDAGE TO YOUR

PAST, FEARFUL OF YOUR PRESENT, AND CONFUSED ABOUT YOUR FUTURE. THE FIRST STEP IN TRANSFORMATION IS TO ACKNOWLEDGE WHERE YOU ARE SPIRITUALLY.

A realist sees both opportunities and obstacles; rebuke and reward. The realist acknowledges Demetrius, the idol maker (Acts 19:24), but chooses to trust in the Holy Spirit for guidance and protection.

REFLECT

Have you ever noticed that for every ten steps forward you seem to take eleven backwards? I hope you know you don't have the monopoly over this. You can still have a spiritual breakthrough. Start by identifying where you are with Christ.

Paul was a realist and one great trait of a realist is to realize you can't do this alone. Once you ask for help, you free God up to act on your behalf and resources will begin to flow toward you. How can God help you right now?

If your mentality is a mess, keep reading. You must reprogram your mind to edify and encourage you on your journey. What is the first step you can take?

DAY 27

THE ADVERSARIES YOU FACE

"…and there are many adversaries."

1 Corinthians 16:9

I have always loved to play sports. Baseball, basketball, football, and golf. I was a pitcher, point guard, quarterback, and in golf, you swing the club. The bottom line is that when I played growing up, I wanted to be actively involved in the game. In all the sports that I participated, I was better than the average player. Realistically, I just thought I was better than what I really was. I grew up playing with (and against) my three older brothers. They did not possess a spirit of compassion, but they drove me to be better even when I was taking a beating. Where I grew up, we played a lot of pick-up games. The team captains alternated to choose their teammates until every player had been picked. Getting chosen last was always demoralizing, even to a kid that was several years younger than his brothers. There was one thing worse than being picked last, and that was sitting on the bench.

Sitting on the bench was awful. I was taught to root for my team and to encourage those playing the game, even when I'm not involved. After a while, the players sitting on the bench would always begin to criticize the players on the field. "We could have made that catch" or "I can't believe he struck out." Do you realize there is nothing worse than a spectator who criticizes? When the game begins to get boring and you begin to criticize those on the field, the many adversaries you face are eliminated down to just one. The adversary you face is you. When doors of opportunity open from the Lord, the adversary of fear, doubt, anxiety, worry, stress, and insecurity come from within not from without. I'm not facing the adversary; the adversary is me. When I surrender to His plan for my life the journey gets exciting. When I decide to exchange my strength, His peace and contentment become fruit produced within me by the Holy Spirit.

TRANSFORMATIONAL TRUTH:
THE CHRISTIAN ADVENTURE IS NEVER BORING!

WHEN YOU DECIDE TO WALK BY FAITH UNDER THE GUIDANCE AND DIRECTION OF THE INDWELLING HOLY SPIRIT, THE JOURNEY TAKES YOU TO PLACES YOU NEVER DREAMED YOU COULD GO. AT TIMES, IT CAN SCARE THE DAYLIGHTS OUT OF YOU. THE CHRISTIAN ADVENTURE ISN'T AN OXYMORON WHEN YOU ARE SEEKING AN ACTIVE, INTIMATE, PERSONAL

Have you ever felt outnumbered? Have you ever felt the odds stacked against you? Paul faced multiple situations where He could have thrown in the towel and quit. Imprisoned, stoned, and left for dead. Shipwrecked, floating in the sea for three days, snake bites, and getting beaten with rods. He even had to be placed in a basket and lowered over a wall to escape those trying to kill him. Did I mention that he spent time in jail? Three times, but who's counting.

Paul had to endure persecution for his testimony to the resurrection of Jesus Christ. The game of life certainly didn't seem fair. How was it that Paul could face each open door as a new opportunity? No matter what life threw at him, Paul learned to be content. He knew what it was like to prosper and he knew how it felt to lose it all. Yet, adversity and adversaries no longer controlled his life. The next time you face adversity look inside first. Make sure the adversary isn't within and trust Him for the strength to walk through the door He has opened for you. Let the adventure begin. Get back on the playing field and enjoy the game.

REFLECT

When you feel you're outnumbered, never forget He has promised to never leave you nor forsake you. I pray you can sense His presence right now.

If your walk with Christ has become boring, will you quit sitting on the bench and tell the coach you're ready to play? When He sees faith, He begins to remove the obstacles in your way.

The Bible declares, "Greater is He that is in you than he that is in the world." It's one thing to acknowledge this as true, but this becomes faith when you believe it is true.

DAY 28

WHEN ADVERSITY HITS HOME

"But I will tarry at Ephesus until Pentecost. For a great and effective door has been opened to me, and there are many adversaries. And if Timothy comes, see that he may be with you without fear; for he does the work of the Lord, as I also do. Therefore let no one despise him. But send him on his journey in peace..."

1 Corinthians 16:9-11

When you think of warfare, you probably think of two opposing armies representing two opposing nations; bearing arms against each other with the purpose of winning the war and hopefully, an eventual peace. Some wars are fought merely for power or to enslave another people. Wars are fought in the name of religion, injustice, geographical boundaries, and the original sin of pride. Whenever one people group thinks they're superior to another, or that one ethnic group is substandard citizens, demonic activity is always involved. Never underestimate the evil that one man or nation is willing to inflict upon another. Impending results of a war fought for personal gain, ambition, or power can be described by one word, Holocaust.

I once heard a joke about a guy that attempted to remain neutral in the Civil War, so he wore a blue shirt and gray pants. What were the results? They shot at him from both sides. I know that is a corny joke, but tragically it's true. At times, you take shrapnel from both sides. There are outward adversaries, some of which can be seen by the naked eye. Paul says that you do not wrestle with flesh and blood, but with principalities and powers from the supernatural realm (Ephesians 6:12-13). You must fight these battles in the supernatural power of the Holy Spirit that dwells in your life. Isn't it amazing that Paul chose to use the analogy of wrestling? Wrestling is hand to hand combat that's close range and can be very violent. I'm not talking about WWF. As a kid, I used to watch Big Time Wrestling that had characters such as Bo-Bo Brazil, the Sheik, and the Kentuckian. It was very entertaining, but it had one major issue: everyone knew that it was "fake" wrestling. It was staged, rehearsed, well-choreographed, and it was a sham. Paul was a realist and dealt with authentic living. Although he was excited about the open door at Ephesus, Paul was acutely aware that the same door of blessing would also open the same portal for adversity and pain.

**TRANSFORMATIONAL TRUTH:
THE MAJORITY OF YOUR SPIRITUAL WARFARE IS
A RESULT OF "FRIENDLY FIRE."**

FRIENDLY FIRE OCCURS WHEN COMMUNICATION
LINES ARE BLURRED, ORDERS ARE NOT FOLLOWED,
OR WRONG COORDINATES ARE GIVEN. TRAGICALLY,
LIVES ARE LOST IN BATTLE AND SOLDIERS WILL BE
SEVERELY WOUNDED OR MAIMED. IT'S HORRIFIC TO
ENGAGE IN WARFARE, BUT IT IS DEVASTATING WHEN
LIVES ARE LOST THROUGH FRIENDLY FIRE.

The truth of the matter is, when you step through an open door, you are immediately hit with friendly fire. Others say why you shouldn't enter the open door, why it won't work, or caution you because the risks are too great. Paul writes to Corinth and says that when Timothy arrives, let him be among you without fear. Let no one despise him. To despise Timothy here means to look down on him or to belittle him. Paul states that he and Timothy were co-laborers together in the work of the Lord. Paul expected to be faced with external adversaries. He understood that taking Ephesus would require hand-to-hand combat. What Paul didn't have time for was the cheap potshots from within. He begged them to send Timothy forward in peace. If you have friendly fire in your life, take action to isolate it or confront it, but never let it be ignored.

REFELCT

How can you take action over the friendly fire in your life right now?

Choose wisely who you allow into your inner circle. Are those closest to you adding value to your life or sucking the life out of you?

Are you a positive influence to those around you and are you adding value to those closest to you? Pour yourself into encouraging others on their journey!

DAY 29

NEVER CHASE YOUR ADVERSARY

*"Watch, stand fast in the faith, be brave, be strong.
Let all that you do be done with love."*

Corinthians 16:13

Have you ever done something incredibly dumb? Maybe it started out as a good idea or you needed something to break the boredom of the day. Then, you realize this reality: "This is gonna hurt!" or "That's gonna leave a mark!" When someone says "Hey, watch this!" and follows it with a "That ain't nothin!" statement, you know the series of events that will follow could scar you for life. I have lived through, and can clearly recall several of those moments.

When I was twelve, we moved to the country. It was traumatic for me to leave behind the only home I had ever known, along with every one of my childhood friends. I was required to change to a rival school, ride a bus for almost an hour, and attempt to "fit in" to an established sports program that was well underway. Adversaries faced me everywhere I went, in all that I did, in my new country life.

I was a city boy who rarely left his yard, now trying to adjust to open fields, camping out, fishing, and walking to the drive-in theater every night to catch a movie. I tried everything I could do to blend in with the crowd. On one such occasion, during my first summer in the country, I went on a fishing and hiking excursion with some friends. We had a very modest home with two acres of land. The family directly behind us had over three hundred acres, with four different ponds, and more woods than I had ever experienced in my short twelve years. It also had a train track that ran through the middle of the property. Being directionally impaired, I made sure to stay close to the guys who I assumed would know their way in and out of the "jungle."

On one of the first encounters with my new friends, we hiked back through the railroad tracks to a tunnel that ran underneath. This was a cylinder tunnel that, at twelve years old, I could almost stand up in. As boys were prone to do, we were always trying to out-do one another. I'll never forget, as we got close to the tunnel, we saw an object moving towards us in the opening. Suddenly, one of the guys yelled: "Let's catch it!" I'd never had much interaction with animals, especially animals in their own territory. I had never even owned a cat or a dog. I once had a goldfish that we had to give a burial at sea, aka we flushed him down the toilet. As a result, I didn't have an arsenal of wisdom or experience. What we thought was a good idea marked my life forever.

As we moved closer, we could see that the animal was a very large groundhog. We picked up some small stones to give it a chase and entered into the tunnel. After getting about halfway through, everything in that area became darker. I could see the light at the opposite end from where we entered. The light was reassuring, and I thought everything appeared to be okay. It was then I heard a sound that I have yet to hear again. A sound that sent chills down my spine and stopped four boys in their tracks. The groundhog decided that he was through running away from us. Alarmed by this change of events, we decided it was time to start running away from him! I can still vividly remember thinking that if I could outrun at least one of the other boys, I would survive. It was every man for himself. The groundhog had us on "his turf," and he wasn't budging. Fortunately, I lived to tell the tale of some dumb, twelve-year-old boys adventure by the railroad track.

**TRANSFORMATIONAL TRUTH:
ALWAYS GIVE PROPER RESPECT TO THE
ADVERSARIES IN YOUR LIFE.**

NOWHERE IN SCRIPTURE ARE WE ADVISED TO CHASE DOWN THE ENEMY, ESPECIALLY INTO HIS TERRITORY. JAMES INSTRUCTED US TO "RESIST THE DEVIL, AND HE WILL FLEE FROM YOU." PAUL WARNED OTHERS OF ADVERSARIES SUCH AS DEMETRIUS AND ALEXANDER THE COPPERSMITH, WHO HAD DONE HIM MUCH

HARM. AS PAUL FACED THE ADVERSARIES, LURKING BEHIND EVERY OPEN DOOR, HE SAID WATCH, STAND FAST, AND BE BRAVE. WHEN YOU'RE IN ENEMY TERRITORY, DON'T GO INTO BATTLE ARMED WITH JUST A FEW SMALL STONES. PUT ON THE WHOLE ARMOR OF GOD (EPHESIANS 6:10-13).

REFLECT

Thank God today for His protection in your dumb moments of the past. He has promised to never leave you nor forsake you.

Ask God to give you a godly respect for the enemy. One that heightens your awareness of his strategy to kill, steal, and destroy.

Will you stop trying to impress others and live for an audience of one? His name is Jesus!

DAY 30

THE DOOR OF THE ADVERSARY

"And it came to pass, when Joshua was by Jericho, that he lifted his eyes and looked and behold, a Man stood opposite him with His sword drawn in His hand. And Joshua went to Him and said to Him, "are you for us or for our adversaries?" So He said, "No, but as Commander of the army of the Lord I have now come." And Joshua fell on his face and worshiped, and said to Him, "What does my Lord say to His servant?" Then the Commander of the Lord's army said to Joshua, "Take your sandal off your foot, for the place where you stand is holy." And Joshua did so. Now Jericho was securely shut up because of the children of Israel; none went out, and none came in."

Joshua 5:13-6:1

As Paul surveyed the situation at Ephesus, he saw tremendous potential. He saw a city that would become a launching pad for missionaries all over the world. This city also held the seemingly, insurmountable wall of idolatry and pagan worship. Idolatry and Emperor worship had a stronghold on the city, to the natural eye, it spelled defeat. Paul knew this would be a spiritual, not physical warfare. Joshua faced a similar situation as the children of Israel had crossed over the Jordan River to claim the land of Canaan. This would be their promised inheritance from the Lord, which dwelt on the plains of Jericho. As an incredible General and leader of the nation of Israel, Joshua goes to scout out the city of Jericho.

Jericho had become renowned for its famed walls, which protected the city from invading armies. Many maneuvered around Jericho, as it held no significant military stature. Invaders did not want to spend the extended time needed to breach the walls, nor was it worth the loss of life and valuable resources. Joshua's first encounter with Israel's Commander in Chief came as he saw a walled, well-fortified enemy. Imagine for a moment Joshua overlooking Jericho, staring intently at those walls, where side-by-side chariot races were held. As Joshua lifts his eyes off the enemy, he is confronted by a soldier with a sword drawn in His hand. He knew that this was no ordinary Man.

TRANSFORMATIONAL TRUTH:
WHEN YOU FACE THE ADVERSARIES OF LIFE,
YOU DON'T HAVE TO FACE THEM ALONE.

GOD NEVER INTENDED YOU TO FACE YOUR ENEMIES ALONE. THIS IS A FAITH OF DEPENDENCY, NOT INDEPENDENCE. THERE WILL BE SOME ADVERSARIES YOU MUST CONFRONT AND TRIALS YOU MUST

GO THROUGH, NOT AROUND. GOD HAS PROMISED TO GO BEFORE YOU! THE COMMANDER IN CHIEF DIDN'T COME TO TAKE SIDES; HE CAME TO TAKE OVER. WHENEVER YOU HAVE AN ENCOUNTER WITH JESUS, AND JESUS CALMS THE STORMS OF LIFE, YOU'RE NEVER THE SAME.

Joshua fell on his face and worshiped. He was ready to serve in any capacity. That might seem extreme, but it wasn't enough. Jesus wants you to know that when He calms the storms and silences adversaries, that's holy ground. When the walls fall down, remember the holiness of the moment! The enemy was already defeated before the walls ever came down. In Joshua 6:2, the Lord said to Joshua, look I have given you the city. Through natural eyes, Joshua was looking at the same fortified doors and the same closed gates. The city was in lockdown. The doors were closed and the people of Jericho were ready to fight. They could hold out for months if necessary. Never forget that what you see as an obstacle, God sees as an opportunity. His methods for tackling your adversaries might seem odd or unusual. Faith always focuses on the way not the wall. Faith sees strongholds as solutions, as demolished rubble in the hands of the Lord. Adversaries roar because that's all they can do!

REFLECT

Adversity comes in the forms of people, places, and things. All these are tools in the hand of Satan. He tries to get our eyes on other people, on things, or on ourselves. What can you do to keep your eyes on Jesus?

Never forget that Jericho, while impressive, was in a posture of defense. Instead of surrounding the children of Israel, Israel surrounded the city. Greater is He that is in us, than he that is in the world.

Did you ever look at your adversaries through the lenses of being on holy ground with God? God deems holy what you view as a hindrance.

DAY 31

I AM MY OWN WORST ENEMY

"…and there are many adversaries."

1 Corinthians 16:9

For nine years, I watched Jaleel White (Steve Urkel) entertain in the sitcom *Family Matters*. This is one of my favorite sitcoms of all time, ranked right up there with *The Andy Griffith Show* and *Happy Days*. Steve Urkel had a way of causing chaos for anyone and everyone that he met. Each week I waited in anticipation for his famous line, "Did I do that?" At the end of each show, everything seemed to work out, and forgiveness was displayed for all to see.

"Did I do that?"
Steve Urkel, Family Matters

131

How many times in your life have you said, "Did I do that?" or "Did I say that?" or maybe, "Did I think that?" What you do, say, or think are the three sins that you battle every day. These formidable adversaries will continually confront you with actions, attitudes, or arrogance. I've had the privilege to be married to my wife Donna for 42 years and counting, but it was anything but love at first sight for her. When we first met at a mutual friend's home, I was "in love." Donna, not so much. I did everything I could think of to impress her, hoping she would at least give me a chance. Just one date. Eight times she gave me a resounding "No!" I decided to take the Steve Urkel approach. If you've forgotten it, let me remind you of his second most famous line: "I'm wearing you down babe!" He desperately tried to swoon his dream girl Laura, and win her heart. I wish I could tell you that I did something extraordinary to convince Donna to go on a date with me, but that would be lying. It was her sister that gave her this advice, "Go out with the guy, it's a free meal!" I became a charity case, but none of that mattered because six months later, we were married. Needless to say, it was an incredible first date. I always tried to be the guy who made everybody laugh, and she saw right through that act. Donna took the time to see the real me.

We've grown together during these last 42 years, but it hasn't always been easy. In fact, at one point in our marriage, it nearly ended. We had been married almost six years when I took my eyes off Jesus and put them on people. For the next four years, I ran from God and made everyone around me miserable. When Donna asked me to leave, I came face-to-face with the worst and most deadly adversary known to mankind: pride. Over the next few months, I felt it raise its ugly head time and time again with the same agenda, to kill, steal, and destroy.

**TRANSFORMATIONAL TRUTH:
REPENTANCE DOESN'T ASK, "DID I DO THAT?"**

GENUINE REPENTANCE SAYS, "I DID DO THAT!" WHEN THIS TRANSFORMATION HAPPENS, HEALING BEGINS, FORGIVENESS IS BOTH RECEIVED AND GIVEN, AND THE MIRACULOUS TAKES PLACE. YOU FREE GOD TO MOVE IN YOUR LIFE, AND IN THE LIVES OF THOSE AROUND YOU.

I am so thankful that God healed my home. It took time, hard work, honest assessments, and intentional communication. No more generic comments like, "Did I do that?" When I set aside my pride, an amazing event took place. We became best friends. Not all stories have a happy ending, and not all marriages can be saved. There are many adversaries that can derail you spiritually. The attack on marriages and homes is at the top of Satan's agenda. It took both of us, allowing the process of repentance to work in us, to see lasting change take place.

REFLECT

If God has done a work of restoration in your life, will you share that with someone today? They may need to hear your story. It may give them hope.

Pride is the original sin. The "blame game" closely follows. If you make an honest assessment today of your spiritual condition with the relationships in your life, are you full of pride?

No amount of hard work and determination can heal your home. This is a spiritual issue that must be solved with a spiritual solution. That solution is repentance.

DAY 32

READY OR NOT, HERE I COME!

"But I will tarry in Ephesus until Pentecost.
For a great and effective door has opened to me,
and there are many adversaries."

1 Corinthians 16:8-9

Did you ever play that game when you were a child? The simple game of hide and go seek? You count to a designated number, usually thirty, and while you were counting the others playing will go and hide. When you've finished counting, you yell with a loud voice: "Ready or not, here I come!" The last person found wins the game. Here is what I learned about the game from having three older brothers; they never came looking! I could hide for hours, or until I had to go to the restroom. As I got older, I began to realize their strategy, and the game quickly lost its appeal.

Whenever God opens a door to expand His kingdom or accelerate your spiritual growth through testing, adversity shouts "Ready or not, here I come!" Adversity isn't an elective; it's a required course. You cannot opt out of the adversaries of life. The Bible even has a term to describe it. Warfare, or in this case, spiritual warfare. Paul planned to remain in Ephesus until Pentecost. At Pentecost, the Holy Spirit descends from Heaven and indwells those who were in the Upper Room. He gives a supernatural power that energizes them to the streets of Jerusalem. Game on! Spiritual warfare has it's beginning at the same time Jesus sent the Holy Spirit to be the helper and comforter. Stephen and James will be martyred and the Osama bin Laden of the nation of Israel, Saul of Tarsus, will go on a rampage. He will assault, imprison, and execute those who are known as "Christians" or as the term means, little Christ's.

TRANSFORMATIONAL TRUTH: SPIRITUAL WARFARE IS A TRUTH TO BE RESPECTED!

THE ENEMY HAS AN ARSENAL OF WEAPONS AT HIS DISPOSAL. WHILE YOU SLEEP TONIGHT HE IS PLANNING YOUR NEXT SET OF TESTS, TRIALS, AND TEMPTATIONS. HE IS RELENTLESS IN HIS PURSUIT, AND HE IS TO BE RESISTED IN THE POWER OF THE HOLY SPIRIT. YOU CAN BE EITHER A CONQUEROR OR A CASUALTY, BUT YOU'RE NEVER A CONSCIENTIOUS OBJECTOR! ONE DAY SOON THE WAR WILL BE OVER. JESUS IS COMING. HEAR HIS CRY, "READY OR NOT, HERE I COME!"

As a believer in Christ, you are now a new creation; created for good works. The goal and agenda are to be salt and light in a dark, decaying, and dying world. There are some Christians who don't understand that once you surrender your life to Jesus, and accept Him as your Savior and Lord, you are now a target of all the forces of evil. Hear again the cry of the adversary, "Ready or not, here I come!" You have been saved by faith in Jesus Christ, and given the Holy Spirit to guide you on this journey. You have God's word as your guide and prayer as your communication system. You have the church to help in the process of discipleship, and to equip you to do the work of the ministry. You have been gifted by the Holy Spirit to serve the body of Christ. You wear a suit of spiritual armor, specifically designed to protect you from the adversaries you face.

"Put on the whole armor of God, that you may be able to stand against the wiles (tactics) of the devil… therefore take up the whole armor of God, that you may be able to withstand in the evil day, and having done all, to stand."

Ephesians 6:11, 13

REFLECT

Spiritual warfare isn't a game! Both Heaven and Hell take it seriously. So should you!

Start each day with the reality that you're in enemy territory. Spiritual, physical, emotional, and financial areas of your life are up for grabs and are tools the enemy will use to get your eyes off Jesus and His promises.

Rest today knowing that Jesus Christ is coming. One day spiritual warfare will be over. Until then stay on the offensive. Be prepared for battle each day.

DAY 33

PROTECTION FROM THE UNKNOWN

*"For a great and effective door has opened to me,
and there are many adversaries."*

1 Corinthians 16:9

A s a teenager, I can remember the exact time and place when I declared to my buddies three things I would never do. The first was one said out of jest; "I'll never work at McDonald's!" At this age, everyone was getting a job, the economy was tough, and my teenage job was secure on the golf course. I started when I was nine, working to play for free. I began working there in a paid capacity when I was fourteen. I would eventually be a supervisor for McDonald's for several years in my twenty's. I was fourteen years old when our pastor resigned. I had seen several pastors resign during my short fourteen years on the planet. My second declaration was that "I will never be a pastor, who would want that job?" I have been a pastor for the last thirty years of my life. The third statement regarded a missionary who shared with our church about his recent trip to Africa. I can distinctly remember looking at my friend and saying, "I'll never go to Africa." I will soon go on my third trip and have been to Cameroon, Equatorial Guinea, the Democratic Republic of Congo, South Africa, Malawi, and briefly in Mozambique.

It was my journey into the Democratic Republic of Congo (DRC) that I learned first-hand about His protection from the unknown adversaries of life. During this seventeen-day mission trip, my team took a couple days of downtime from the hectic pace to see some of the country. Our missionary told us of a DRC safari he had always wanted to go on and found a pilot who could take us there. I was very skeptical about the trip, but my wife was all-in! Looking back, I am certain that she was momentarily demon-influenced. We arrived at a very small airport which meant only one thing: a very small airplane. I soon realized that I must be a prophet. There were five of us, plus the pilot, getting on a six-seat airplane, held together with duct tape. We went through a weight screening to find the total for the six flyers. Once we had the official weigh-in, the pilot placed a box on the scale and said, "We're not going anywhere until we lose fifty-two pounds in that box." Bottom line is this. We took the clothes on our back, drivers licenses', passports, and a bottle of water each upon our missionaries' insistence. I had to leave everything else behind in an airport locker, even my belt! My wife was like a preschooler who had just seen a swing-set for the first time. Due to my physical condition, specifically my legs, I had the privilege to sit next to the pilot for the most legroom available. Donna and a female church member sat in the second row. While our missionary and a gentleman from our church sat crammed in the back of the plane. They were all packed in tight like a TV dinner.

TRANSFORMATIONAL TRUTH:
GOD'S UNSEEN HAND IS ALWAYS
PROTECTING YOU!

WHEN YOU EMBARK ON JOURNEY'S THAT YOU DIDN'T ANTICIPATE, AND FACE UNEXPECTED ADVERSARIES, HIS SUSTAINING GRACE GOES WITH YOU. THERE IS NO SAFER PLACE TO BE THAN IN THE CENTER OF HIS WILL.

As the plane took off, I began a conversation with a brilliant, very young, missionary pilot. After some small talk, I asked about the length of this trip; he had been quite insistent upon everyone using the rest-room before we were airborne. He informed me that the flight was about two hours and forty-five minutes to a very remote area, where we would be landing on a grass runway. This safari lodge was only accessible by air or boat. I had never flown over a jungle before, and after about forty-five minutes, I began to notice that this was the real deal. The only break in the trees was an occasional river. I then asked a question that would teach me about the unseen hand of God. "I don't see much in the way of civilization below. Where would we land if the single-engine plane had mechanical trouble?" The pilot answered the question almost immediately as if he had anticipated or heard my questions before. "There's plenty of places to land, but it hurts when you do." To be continued…

REFLECT

How many times can you recall God protecting you after the fact?

Never tell God what you will "never" do, even if you're kidding! He has a marvelous sense of humor.

I wonder, how many things would have happened had He not protected me? Take a moment and thank Him right now for His unseen hand guarding your life.

DAY 34

NO PLACE TO LAND,
NO PLACE TO RUN!

"…and there many adversaries."

1 Corinthians 16:9

Our flight continued as I kept one eye on the engine and one eye on the ground. I was trying to spot places where we could land, if necessary. Most people wouldn't ask any more questions, but I've never been that bright. When I asked about the duct tape holding the plane together, the pilot went on to describe how one of his more hazardous duties was to help evacuate missionaries during times of civil war or persecution. On one recent adventure, he landed and quickly loaded a mom and six children with an immediate takeoff. The pilot went back two more times to evacuate personnel to which he then made this statement, "The rebels were getting better at shooting the third time." That's when I realized the planes duct tape was covering bullet holes. A major lesson about the unseen hand of God.

As we approached the end of our journey, I heard an audible moan from the back of the plane as the pilot announced we would be landing soon. They were all ready to land. I watched as we flew over the jungle, a river, a village, and then a grass runway. It was something right out of National Geographic! We pulled to the end of the grass runway to a very crudely formed shelter. As we approached the end of the runway, people began to walk out of the jungle to greet us. Needless to say, we were glad to be on the ground. The thought of the return flight quickly faded as we met the indigenous people and the children as our pilot took off. We made our walk to the lodge on the Sangha River, and I listened to the sound of the real jungle. I had been in Africa, but never to a place like this. The sound of the monkeys was incredible. I walked by an ant-hill that was three feet taller than I am, and I'm six feet two inches tall! These were ants on steroids. They escorted us down a small cleared trail to our hut which rested on eight-foot stilts to protect against the rising river during the rainy season. As we entered, we saw beds with mosquito netting, and I knew I was "in" Africa. The deck view of the river was breathtaking. I was in awe of God's creation. As Donna and I went to leave the hut, we saw the only English sign in the entire village, mounted to the back of the hut's front door. It said: "Please stay on the path due to the vipers." It donned on me that we weren't "in Kansas anymore."

**TRANSFORMATIONAL TRUTH:
NEVER UNDERESTIMATE THE VALUE OF
INTERCESSORY PRAYER IN YOUR LIFE.**

DONNA AND I WERE PRAYED FOR DAILY BY ABOUT
TWO HUNDRED PRAYER WARRIORS. PAUL BEGGED, IN
EVERY LETTER HE WROTE, FOR PEOPLE TO PRAY FOR
HIM AND REMEMBER HIM IN HIS CHAINS. HE KNEW
THAT HE WOULD BE ATTACKED FROM THE OBVI-
OUS AND THE UNKNOWN. HE NEEDED PROTECTION
FROM BOTH!

As we made our way to the Sangha River for dinner, we sat under a straw hut overlooking this magnificent river. That's when I first saw the eagles and I made a comment to our missionary about their beauty. He mumbled something to our waiter and they both laughed. I realized that they were not only laughing near me, they were also laughing at me. I asked our missionary what he had said to the waiter; he replied that he never viewed the bats as beautiful before. As we ate our meal that night, the bats would swoop over our table. Their three-to-four foot wingspan was quite impressive. Needless to say, I didn't eat very much that evening. I don't even like American bats let alone bats that can rearrange furniture. This was another trust test for me, and I was failing miserably. And the story continues…

REFLECT

God protects you from dangers both seen and unseen. He is faithful. Trust in His protection and faithfulness.

I need people praying and interceding for me every day, not just while I am on a missionary trip to Africa. Who can you be praying for?

Jesus had Peter, James, and John that He prayed with. Do you know of three people that are praying for you?

DAY 35

WHAT YOU CAN'T SEE CAN HURT YOU

"… we wrestle not against flesh and blood…"

Ephesians 6:12

After surviving the "bat dinner" and the "viper trail," I surprisingly got a great night's rest. We began our day with an exciting boat ride, in a hollowed-out log, to visit a pygmy village about forty minutes north on the Sangha River. The log was powered by two guides who stood on each end of the boat. They held long poles to maneuver us through the swift current. The next near-death adventure involved an adversary I didn't see but heard. When you think of a safari what comes to your mind? Here is how I had visualized our day to unfold. We would enter a safari jeep, take a guided tour through the game reserve, and see every sort of animal I had observed on TV wild-life shows.

We did enter a jeep and began the drive to what I assumed was a game reserve. After driving for about an hour, we finally pulled off "the road" and parked alongside a river. Our guide spoke no English, was about five feet tall, and weighed about ninety pounds soaking wet with rocks in his pocket. Thankfully our missionary was able to communicate with him. Our guide took off his flip flops and proceeded to wade into the river. The river was approximately twenty feet wide and lined on both sides with bulrushes. We proceeded to roll up our jeans and take our shoes and socks off, tying them around our neck so they wouldn't get wet. The water was never deeper than three and one-half feet, but keeping our jeans dry wasn't going to be an option. We waded through the river for about a half mile before we saw a trail. After putting our shoes back on, we walked for about three miles.

I had seen the jungle from the air and on the movies, but this was so dense that at one point it began to rain, and we weren't getting wet. Our guide gave us some basic instructions on what to do in case we encountered any wild animals. This safari was the Zoo without the cages! As we neared the end of our three-mile hike, we came to a clearing where we climbed several flights of wooden stairs. This opened up into a large observation platform, overlooking a muddy watering hole. We saw about thirty-five elephants and multiple animal clusters. The animals walked out of the jungle in groups and left as a group. I guess they felt that there was strength in numbers. It was a breathtaking sight. After about three hours, our guide said we had to leave. The grazing animals would soon make their way to the river. We needed to start our way back first, or we would not get out until the next morning.

We reentered the river to begin our journey back to the jeep. We were wading through with our guide and our missionary in the front of the line. They were followed by myself, with my wife and another couple from our church bringing up the rear. That's when it happened. A couple of times I had thought I saw something moving in the bulrushes. It was like seeing a mouse in your home, wondering if you actually saw it at all. I asked our missionary what could be making the noise. After corresponding with the guide, he stayed silent. I took a few more steps and then hesitantly asked, "What did he say?" Our missionary slowly turned to say "The crocodiles aren't aggressive!" He wasn't kidding. What you can't see really can hurt you!

TRANSFORMATIONAL TRUTH:
YOU MUST WALK BY FAITH, NOT BY SIGHT!

NOT ALL SAFARI EXPEDITIONS ARE THE SAME. EVERYONE FACES THE REALITY OF HAVING THE LIFE SCARED OUT OF THEM. SOMETIMES, YOU'RE BETTER OFF NOT SEEING THE ADVERSARIES YOU FACE. ONE THING I HAVE LEARNED ON THIS CHRISTIAN ADVENTURE IS THAT, IF IT'S NOT MY TIME TO GO HOME, NOTHING WILL TAKE ME THERE. IF IT IS MY TIME TO GO, NOTHING ON THIS EARTH WILL KEEP ME HERE. AS YOU RIDE THIS JOURNEY CALLED LIFE, LOOK OUT THE WINDOW AND ENJOY THE VIEW.

REFLECT

Have you ever looked back and said, "I don't know how I survived that!" You now have your answer: God!

You cannot factor out faith in your life. Without faith, it is impossible to please Him.

Had I known what adversaries were a part of our safari, I probably would have stayed back, but then missed watching God's creation play in the mud.

DAY 36

LET GOD HANDLE YOUR ADVERSARIES

"...and there are many adversaries."

1 Corinthians 16:9

In every neighborhood and school, there is an adversary. Somebody bigger than you. Someone who doesn't like you. Someone that the old expression "has your number" fits. They intimidate, heckle, and harass you. Sometimes it's deserved, but more than not it's undeserved. I grew up in a rough section of Hamilton, OH, known as Armondale. I had my fair share of physical adversaries. Spiritual adversaries abounded everywhere, but at this point on my young journey, the physical was the most intimidating.

When I turned ten, I bought my first bicycle from Bowden's Bicycle shop. I worked and did chores for almost a year to earn enough money to buy this used, yet new to me, bike. I was thankful that I could now ride my bike to little league practice. My team was the Dollar Federal Pirates, and I was thrilled to get started. There was one problem. I had to ride my bike down a street where my arch enemy lived. I still have never figured out why I was his designated, seemingly favorite, target. I had to face this reality three times per week. I was riding along one morning as fast my bony legs could peddle this three-speed bike. Suddenly, I felt this sharp stinging pain in my left cheek (the one not attached to my face). I had been the victim of a BB gun shot, and this kid was accurate. Being target practice each week gave me great sympathy for those ducks at the county fair shooting gallery.

I started to wear two pairs of shorts under my baseball uniform, a sweatshirt, Elmer Fudd style hat and my dad's safety goggles three days per week. I took the treacherous journey because, in my mind, little league was worth the temporal pain. Then it happened. It was a Saturday morning and I had just returned from the weekly laundry mat ritual with mom. I was sitting on the front porch and off in the distance I could see a rather large, imposing figure riding a bike, some eight sizes too small, for his Herculean frame. I soon realized that my adversary was on my turf, and revenge was the name of the game. I didn't own a BB Gun, but my brother did, and he wasn't home. My plan to execute a measure of revenge was in play. I had dreamed of this moment for weeks, played out every scenario in my head, and all of them were sweet. Now, Goliath was riding directly past the front of my house and today was reckoning day. I was in the mindset of David from the Old Testament. To all of Israel, Goliath was too big to hit; David thought Goliath was too big to miss! Since he was eight times my size, I had to execute this sniper, unseen, premeditated plan without fail.

Our home had an old coal chute that went directly into our basement. We no longer used it since dad had upgraded to an oil furnace. There was a black iron door that was propped open with a stick. It was the perfect set-up! I pointed the barrel of my BB Gun through the opening. As my adversity rode by, I followed him with the BB Gun until I thought I had the perfect angle. As I moved with the target, my BB Gun hit the stick which slammed shut the iron door. I had shot my Dad's car window! I was horrified as I watched the glass crack into a million different pieces. Oh boy, was I going to be in trouble.

TRANSFORMATIONAL TRUTH:
LET GOD TAKE CARE OF YOUR ADVERSARIES.

IF YOU ATTEMPT TO CONFRONT ADVERSARIES ON YOUR OWN, KNOW THAT YOUR SIN WILL FIND YOU OUT! WHENEVER I TAKE SOMEONE TO THE DIVINE WOODSHED, I FIND OUT THAT GOD IS WAITING FOR BOTH OF US. RELAX AND ALLOW GOD TO FIGHT YOUR BATTLES FOR YOU. IF NOT, YOU'LL FACE THE WRATH OF YOUR FATHER. THE BB THAT HIT MY CHEEK (NOT ON MY FACE) PALED IN COMPARISON TO MY FATHER'S BELT!

REFLECT

I look back on this story with great amusement, but it wasn't funny at the time. The trial you're facing will soon pass and you will learn the lesson your Father teaches you.

What adversary do you need to release to the Lord right now? Please take my advice: They're not worth the anxiety in your life. Release them to the Lord.

Goliath was a defeated foe when David picked up five smooth stones from the creek-bed. Allow the Goliath's in your life to be seen through the lens of scripture.

DAY 37

NOT EVERY ADVERSARY IS AN ADVERSARY

"…and there are many adversaries."

1 Corinthians 16:9

D o you have a favorite teacher or coach who sticks out in your mind? I certainly do! I also have a not-so-favorite teacher and coach. I'm sure they look back on me as a not-so-favorite student. When I was in the fourth grade, I had an incredible teacher who could see past my attention deficit disorder. Remember, when I had it as a kid it wasn't yet diagnosed. For the most part, my momma simply beat it out of me. The fifth grade was a different story! I had a strict disciplinarian who had a cut and dry, "no bend, no break" policy. If you crossed the line, which I of course did, there was a price to pay. I don't believe I had any recess time that entire year and I had supervised visits to the water fountain and restroom. It was during the fifth grade that I took an empty pellet gun cylinder to school and told the kids it was a bomb. Note to self: that was an extremely bad idea. They evacuated the school and both my parents showed up. Neither was wearing a happy face. I paid dearly for that "duh" moment, and rightfully so!

Much to my surprise, I survived and moved on to the sixth grade. I approached this school year with fear and trembling. It was already tough, since my two brothers had left for the military during the Viet Nam War. One brother departed in the fifth grade, and the second left at the beginning of grade six. This year also brought the new experience of walking through the door of puppy love. You can believe me when I say it felt real to this puppy. In the typical Tom fashion, the young girl I was infatuated with didn't even know I was alive. She was a tom-boy, and I was an above average athlete. If sports weren't around, I didn't exist. I decided to try the routine of being the class clown to get her attention. It would fail miserably.

School hadn't been in session for very long when I tried my first stunt. It would change the course of my life. During a restroom break, I decided to try and hide for the next forty-five minutes until the lunch dismissal. The plan was to stay in the back of the room and hide behind a filing cabinet that sat in front of the bookshelves. Everything was going well for about ten minutes when the one-sided affection of my puppy love suddenly appeared around the filing cabinet. Just before handing me a note from my teacher, she looked me over and rolled her eyes. That permanently closed the door that I thought would lead to love, but I didn't know that another door was opening.

TRANSFORMATIONAL TRUTH:
NOT EVERYONE YOU MEET IS AN ADVERSARY.

ONE BAD EXPERIENCE DOES NOT TAINT THE ENTIRE HUMAN RACE. WHAT I HAD ASSUMED WAS GOING TO BE A DISASTER, TURNED OUT TO BE ONE OF THE MOST GROWING, EYE-OPENING, STRETCHING, AND LEARNING MOMENTS IN MY LIFE. A HANDWRITTEN NOTE AND AN ALTERNATIVE COURSE OF PUNISH-MENT ARE STILL SHAPING MY LIFE TODAY. SOME ADVERSARIES POINT YOU TO NEW OPTIONS!

My teacher's note was direct, simple, and non-negotiable. Here is what it said: "Dear Tommy, please select a book off of the shelves behind you, read it, and write a one-page report about what you've learned. Please rejoin the class after our lunch break together." That got my attention since very few people ever called me Tommy. Generally, my Mom was the only one who could get away with calling me by that name. I can remember pulling out a few books until I found one with a helicopter, dangling ladder, and floodwaters nearly covering a house. The book was entitled, "When the Dikes Broke" by Alta Halverson Seymore, describing a flood that occurred in 1953, Holland. I know you can't judge a book by its cover, but this book helped change my life. I now read on average one book per week. It was my teacher, Nancy Huddleston, who changed my view of the world forever by introducing me to the wonder of reading.

I am eternally grateful that Ms. Huddleston didn't make me walk to the front of the class and take my seat that day. I would have deserved the laughter and embarrassment that my peers were sure to dish out. She demonstrated grace to me. In Sunday school the following week, our teacher asked us to give an example of grace in our lives. That was my example. It was real because I had lived it.

REFELCT

Not all of your adversaries are your enemies. Will you allow God to teach you how to discern between an enemy and a friend?

Try and look at things in a different way. How can you help others see the world from God's point of view? You may be a piece that leads to change in their lives for eternity.

If you struggle in any one area of weakness, read how others have faced it, defeated it, or are still in the process. You don't have to try and solve things on your own.

DAY 38

HE'S BEEN THERE BEFORE

"...and there are any adversaries."

1 Corinthians 16:9

Our nation is still reeling from the effects of Hurricane Michael. Cities gone, lives lost, destruction everywhere. The estimation for recovery efforts is at three to four years. For the most part, people don't think of the weather as an adversary, but Paul experienced it firsthand.

"...Three times I was shipwrecked; a night and a day I have been in the deep...in perils in water...in perils in the sea."

2 Corinthians 11:25, 26

In 2018, the weather channel does an incredible job of providing several days advance warning for storms, especially hurricanes. As you have just seen, even the most modern system cannot anticipate how quickly a storm will intensify, which sometimes means you have to ride it out. Jesus sent His disciples into one such storm on the Sea of Galilee. I once took a boat ride on a replica ship that had been excavated off the bottom of the Sea of Galilee. I can tell you first-hand that it is a breathtaking sight. Surrounded by hills on every side, the storm's come over the mountains quickly and intensify at an accelerated pace. The small vessels of Jesus' day were at the mercy of the storm. Jesus directed His disciples into the boat and told them to go to the other side.

> *"Now it happened on a certain day, that Jesus got into a boat with His disciples. And Jesus said to them, 'Let us cross over to the other side of the lake.' And they launched out."*
>
> *Luke 8:22*

The disciples, being in the perfect will of the Lord, instantly obeyed the request of Jesus. They did not argue, question, or debate His request. They obeyed. Why not? In certain aspects, it was all very familiar to them. Peter, James, and John were professional fisherman who had sailed these waters all their lives. During your Christian adventure, there are storms that you cause, storms that others cause, and storms that God causes. As they began to sail the route to the land of the Gadarenes, a storm arose swiftly, violently, and the scripture declared they were in jeopardy!

Jesus found a quiet place in the back of the boat to rest. This is a true display of Jesus' humanity as

He becomes exhausted in His trials against spiritual warfare. A "windstorm" hit and the boat was covered with waves (Mt. 8:24). These professional fishermen exhausted every resource they had, and yet the ship was still in trouble. You can be in the perfect center of His will, and still be covered by the storm. The narrative changes when one of the men remembers that Jesus is in the boat.

TRANSFORMATIONAL TRUTH:
WHEN THE STORMS OF LIFE HIT, WHY DO YOU FORGET ABOUT JESUS?

JESUS IS IN THE BOAT, ASLEEP, AND THE STORM ISN'T WAKING HIM! WHAT WOKE JESUS? THE CRY OF ONE OF HIS DISCIPLES, "MASTER, WE'RE PERISHING!" HE'S WAITING FOR YOU TO CALL OUT HIS NAME: JESUS. THE NAME OF JESUS CAN CALM YOUR STORM. HE CAN DO MORE IN A BREATH THAN YOU CAN DO IN A LIFETIME.

What Jesus does next is a classic. He gets up, surveys the situation, and rebukes the wind! In my humanity, I'm screaming "you don't drown in the wind, you drown in water!" Jesus always speaks to the source of the problem. The wind was the source, the water was secondary. Allow Jesus to put His finger on the source of your storm today. When He calms your storm, you're never the same.

REFLECT

Jesus told the disciples, "Let *us* go over to the other side." If Jesus is in your boat, it isn't going down!

Jesus has been through every storm that you face, including death. He knows what it's like to face the worst the enemy can throw at Him. He's been there before so you can trust Him.

Where is your faith? In your talent, professionalism, or your portfolio? When the storms of life hit, run to Jesus as fast as you can. If you lose focus, keep looking as He walks on the water to reach you. Allow Him to say, "Peace, be still" to your storm.

DAY 39

THROUGH THE STORM

"…and there are many adversaries."

1 Corinthians 16:9

In 1993, I had an opportunity that came in the form of a phone call. I had a good friend who served as a tour host for a Christian cruise. He invited me to be a last-minute cruise guest since his wife was unable to join him this time. We are both avid golfers, so he had me sold on going within a few minutes. It was January, about ten degrees below zero in Ohio, and we were leaving to play golf on three different islands in the Bahamas. Let me take a moment to pray about it: YES! I felt an immediate answer to that prayer, and my wife gave her nod of approval. In two days, I departed for the airport to fly into Miami and to board the ship. I had never sailed on a cruise, and now this was an exciting reality.

After nearly missing my flight due to a traffic jam, I settled into a very relaxing, smooth journey. I couldn't wait to get boarded, find my room, and begin a new adventure. As we went to our muster station that day to get emergency event instructions, I was impressed by the detail given to all aspects of the ship. The décor, lighting, entertainment, and even the evacuation plan were impressive (although I prayed we wouldn't have to use it). As we departed the port to the cheers of onlookers, I thought "man, this is the life."

We were in the second seating, 8:00 pm dinner. I generally don't eat that late but didn't mind after a hectic day of travel. I had never been to the sea on a large vessel, in the middle of open waters. I did not have any issue up to this point as I had been walking around, getting acclimated to the vessel, and asking a thousand questions. When I sat down for dinner, the first storm hit. I was seated with my pastor and his wife from my home church, along with a few other members that I hadn't seen in a couple of years since going into my first pastorate. After the initial greetings ended, this storm hit without warning. It had been lurking just beneath the surface. Suddenly, I was face first in my empty plate. I still thank God to this day that I did not plunge face-first into any food. I hit the plate with a sound that immediately got everyone's attention, followed by an eruption of laughter. They weren't laughing at me; they were laughing near me. Fortunately, Dramamine came to the rescue after crawling back to my stateroom. I was fine one moment, and face first into my plate the next.

The remainder of the cruise was wonderful. The golf was incredible, the ocean was crystal clear, and the day on the private island was as close to Heaven on Earth as possible. As we began our trip back to the port of Miami, storm clouds on the horizon sent a clear signal that our return voyage would be different. By midnight, we were in what I thought was a full-blown storm of biblical proportions. As I listened to the "sound of many waters" that the ocean created, I knew that noise would always remain etched in my mind. The white-capped waves captivated my attention as I stood on the top deck, letting the rain soak me through. After what seemed like an hour I went back inside and met a couple of crew members. They were surprisingly calm. I asked them about the severity of the storm, and they assured me that it was not as bad as it seemed. They told me that "the captain has been here before." They had learned to trust their captain during the storm. This trip would lead to many more cruises and adventures that my wife and I still enjoy today. I have a saying that "When the ministry gets tough, the tough should go on a cruise!"

**TRANSFORMATIONAL TRUTH:
NOTHING WILL EVER SURPRISE GOD.**

YOU WILL NEVER ENDURE ANY STORM OR ADVERSITY THAT WILL TAKE THE FATHER, SON, AND HOLY SPIRIT BY SURPRISE. THEY NEVER GO INTO EMERGENCY SESSION AND SAY TO ONE ANOTHER, "I DIDN'T SEE THAT COMING!" IN MY TIME ON THIS CHRISTIAN CRUISE, I LEARNED THAT I COULD TRUST THE CAPTAIN. DURING THIS CHRISTIAN ADVENTURE CALLED LIFE, YOU CAN TRUST THE SAVIOR! HE WILL NEVER LEAVE YOU, NOR FORSAKE YOU.

REFLECT

When I stopped looking at the storm and listened to the voice of the crew, the storm lost its intensity. Focus on the One who created the storm today!

When a storm takes you by surprise, it hasn't taken the Lord by surprise. Enjoy the journey even if you're getting drenched!

If Jesus can speak peace to the storm, will you listen to Him to speak into your storm today? He may not choose to calm the waves, but He may calm His child.

VII

THE DOORS YOU FACE

When God closes a door, He is not holding out on you. He has something better planned.

.

DAY 40

SHARE WHAT CHRIST HAS DONE

"Now when they had come and gathered the church together, they reported all that God had done with them, and that He had opened the door of faith to the Gentiles. So they stayed there a long time with the disciples."

Acts 14:27-28

Our forty-day journey together is coming to an end, but please know that as you walk *Through the Door,* the journey has just begun. Share what God has done in your life through this devotional. Paul couldn't contain himself as he shared with the church at Antioch, an exciting new door of faith open in his life. Faith kicked down the closed door of religion and opened the door to an unreached people group, known as the Gentiles. If you're not of Jewish heritage and bloodline, you're a Gentile. Today, in the church, there are no barriers to faith. There are no walls to peak over, and no doors that are racially closed. Whoever calls upon the Name of the Lord will be saved, Jew or Gentile, male or female, slave or free. The door is forever open through the death, burial, and resurrection of Jesus Christ.

What door has God used in your life during this journey of transformation? I would love to hear that he used every door with every reader. In reality, there was probably one that encouraged or challenged you the most. Pass on that blessing to others. Allow the truth to flow through you. Your life is to be a river of blessings, not a reservoir or holding tank. If it was the open door, hear Him once again call your name as He knocks on the door of your heart. If your journey has set you free, please don't keep it inside. Tell someone what He's done for you!

If you walked through the door of salvation, know that all of Heaven is rejoicing with you! I walked through that door fifty-four years ago. As an eight-year-old boy, I began my eternal journey with Christ. What a ride it has been. I never dreamed that a boy from Armondale would travel all over the world telling people about Jesus! As I am in the last one-third of my journey on Earth, I still haven't gotten over the feeling to be set free. It seems like it happened yesterday. Remember, there is always the next day with Jesus! You are still traveling on this journey.

Maybe your fellowship with the Holy Spirit has been renewed. You heard the cry "fore!" and you took that warning seriously. Now that Jesus has your attention, you must keep your eyes on Christ. If you place your eyes on things, people, or yourself, you're destined to fall. If He's still knocking, what are you waiting on? Answer the door. Jesus already has your resume, and He wants your honesty. You can be hard of hearing, even tired of hearing, but He'll keep knocking. There are some voices you can ignore, but His voice isn't one of them.

If your marriage, integrity, and honor remained intact as you ran from the door of sexual immorality, stay close to Jesus, your spouse, and family. The attacks aren't over until He calls you home and you experience Him *after these things* of Earth. The enemy is relentless in his pursuit of your failure. He doesn't get discouraged. Stay on the offensive, build as many memories as you can with your spouse. On the other side, you'll be glad you did! You can take God at His word; we will enjoy Heaven together for all eternity.

The door of adversity is where many reside. The storms you cause will linger; the storms others cause, you endure; the storms God causes you experience. On one of my low days in a hospital room in Tampa, Fl, I didn't go to therapy. I was in pain, discouraged, and far from home. I was alone while my family was fifteen hundred miles away in Ohio. My doctor came to my room and asked what was going on. He told me I could lay here in bed and be in pain, or I could get up and go to therapy and be in pain. Either way, the pain would remain. Transformation sometimes feels a lot like that statement. I'm glad I decided to get on with the journey, face the door of adversity head-on, and keep growing. Choose to move forward in the transformational process. It won't be boring!

REFLECT

If God has used this book to touch your life, rejoice! Send me a note so I can celebrate with you.

If God has used this book to transform you on your journey, share it with your pastor or accountability partner.

If you walked through the door of salvation, tell those in your sphere of influence about the grace you've experienced!

NOTES

Amazing Grace. copyright © 1779. Written by: John Newton

More of You. Gaither Vocal Band, copyright © 1996. Written by: Gary S. Paxton, Gloria Gaither, William J. Gaither

He's Still Working On Me. The Hemphills, copyright © 1980. Written by: Joel Hemphill

Snow White and the Seven Dwarfs. copyright © 1938 by Walt Disney Productions

The Message, copyright © 1993, 1994, 1995, 1996, 2000, 2001, 2002. Used by permission of NavPress Publishing Group.

Exploring Proverbs, John Phillips, copyright © 2002. Kregel Academic.

ACKNOWLEDGMENTS

To my Lord and Savior Jesus Christ whose walked by my side since I was eight! I have no greater title than to be a servant of the King.

Donna – Thanks for not giving up on me when I had given up on myself.

Jessica and Mike – Jess I always treasure our time together, especially our marathon Christmas shopping day! Mike, thanks for loving my daughter unconditionally.

Vanessa – I'll always be in your corner praying for you and for R.J.

Landon, Katie, and my great-grandson Malakai; Carson, Rylan, and Emma you make me smile.

Alianna – It has been a joy and privilege to be grandfather and father at the same time. You keep me young.

Urbancrest Baptist Church – The greatest honor of my life in ministry is to be your pastor. I am still amazed that I get paid to do this. One thing is for certain, it hasn't been boring.

Alex Farmer – Thanks for changing careers from teaching and being a pastry chef, to my executive ministry assistant, and for encouraging me to write. I'll buy you a life-time supply of red pens.

David Bickers – I have no one that I trust more. Thanks for serving alongside me at Urbancrest for twenty years.

My Staff – I have one of the greatest teams ever assembled. Thanks for buying into the vision of serving and investing our lives on others and His Kingdom. You do all the work and I get the credit. It's a great system. You stretch me, keep me young, and intercede for me. I am forever in your debt.